The Mini Rough Guide to
LONDON

YOUR TAILOR-MADE TRIP
STARTS HERE

Tailor-made trips and unique adventures crafted by local experts

HOW ROUGHGUIDES.COM/TRIPS WORKS

STEP 1
Pick your dream destination, tell us what you want and submit an enquiry.

STEP 2
Fill in a short form to tell your local expert about your dream trip and preferences.

STEP 3
Our local expert will craft your tailor-made itinerary. You'll be able to tweak and refine it until you're completely satisfied.

STEP 4
Book online with ease, pack your bags and enjoy the trip! Our local expert will be on hand 24/7 while you're on the road.

PLAN AND BOOK YOUR TRIP AT ROUGHGUIDES.COM/TRIPS

How to download your Free eBook

1. Visit **www.roughguides.com/free-ebook** or scan the **QR code** opposite

2. Enter the code **london894**

3. Follow the simple step-by-step instructions

For troubleshooting contact: mail@roughguides.com

southeastern

Hop on board a Southeastern train and discover Kent

Only a short train ride from London, there is something for everyone to enjoy!

Royal Tunbridge Wells

Canterbury

Margate

Where will you go by train?

Scan here to buy your Advance tickets. No booking fees apply. **The earlier you book, the cheaper the fare.***

*T&Cs apply. Advance tickets are available as single tickets on selected routes at specific times and are subject to availability. For more information, visit southeasternrailway.co.uk/advance

Contents

- **6** **Introduction**
  - 12 10 Things not to miss
  - 14 A perfect day in London
  - 16 The best of London Bridge
  - 18 A day out around Greenwich
- **20** **History**
- **33** **Places**
  - 33 Westminster
  - 42 The West End
  - 49 Buckingham Palace and Mayfair
  - 54 Bloomsbury and Marylebone
  - 60 The South Bank
  - 71 The City
  - 78 Kensington and Chelsea
  - 88 North London
  - 90 East London
  - 94 Southeast London
  - 97 Southwest London
- **101** **Things to do**
  - 101 Shopping
  - 105 Culture
  - 108 Nightlife
  - 110 Outdoor activities
  - 111 Children
  - 112 Festivals and events
- **114** **Food and drink**
- **134** **Travel essentials**
- **148** **Index**

Introduction

London is steeped in history and unmatched character – its skyline a jagged, glimmering contrast of old and new, its distinct neighbourhoods full of unique charm, its iconic streets grey, quaint or thriving with spirited vitality. There's nowhere else quite like it. And in and amongst it all, several vast, green, well-manicured parks make you momentarily forget you're in the thick of a sprawling metropolis.

There's so much to see and experience in London that it can be overwhelming for visitors to figure out where to start. Central London is compact and fun to explore on foot (you can cover more ground walking than you might think) or by bus, bike or tube – the expansive, improving transport system (one of the largest in the world) means that there are usually numerous ways to get from A to B, and on the whole, everything is easily reachable.

South Bank street performer

At the top of most visitors' lists are the city's celebrated landmarks, such as Big Ben, Buckingham Palace, Westminster Abbey, the Tower of London and the London Eye, as well as a fleet of world-class museums, theatres and attractions – a boast of cultural offerings second to none. London's food and drink scene is not to be missed, either – you can eat your way through a cornucopia of cuisine from around the world, from

WHAT'S NEW

London's museum scene is like no other and has welcomed a raft of new, exciting immersive exhibitions in recent years that are changing the way we experience art. Notably, places like the spectacular FRAMELESS museum, opened in 2022, and the internationally renowned Moco Museum, opened in 2024, both by Marble Arch (see page 80), as well as the Lightroom gallery in King's Cross (see page 57), and other fun optical illusion museums like Twist on Oxford Street and the Paradox Museum in Kensington are enjoyable days out.

The food and drink scene in London has taken a few years to recover since the devastating closures and job losses of the Covid pandemic, but it's once again thriving. There's a growing number of Michelin-starred restaurants (80 in London as of 2024), a host of innovative new eateries offering worldly cuisine at places like Greek *Oma* in Borough Market (see page 128) and Japanese *Kinoya* in the recently refurbished Harrods Dining Hall (see page 133), that complement the city's longstanding establishments. There are also several buzzy new food markets dotted across the city (see page 119).

artfully prepared, Michelin-star meals to hearty street food, dipping in and out of the city's famous pubs, bars, restaurants and markets.

POPULATION

After decades of decline, London's population has increased since the mid-1980s to its present 8.9 million and it's forecast to continue growing. London is Europe's most ethnically diverse city and one of the most multicultural cities in the world, with a long, centuries-old immigration history. The various neighbourhoods reflect London's rich cultural make-up and are home to communities with diverse backgrounds such as France, Poland, Ukraine, Africa, the Caribbean, Vietnam, Afghanistan, India and more.

Yet United Kingdom's capital is not without its problems. The basic cost of living – from food prices to travel and rent – is

Black taxi in bustling Piccadilly Circus

incredibly high compared with that in many other capitals, and London is listed as one of the ten most expensive cities in the world. The wealth disparity across the capital is evident, too, with around a quarter of the population living in poverty. The 'Big Smoke' also has its major pollution concerns owing to traffic congestion, although taxes from the 'congestion charge' and the recently expanded 'low emission zone' schemes have reduced casual traffic during peak hours and raised funds for the public transport system. But the city still maintains its allure, a combination of history and opportunity, culture and excess.

AN ORGANIC CITY

Take your time in London and focus on a few key areas or sights because it's impossible to see everything in one trip. Apart from the city's vast size, its long and venerable past is sometimes hidden from view. Over the centuries the ripples of history have repeatedly destroyed parts of the city, and the subsequent rebuilding has resulted in a cocktail of styles laid out over a maze of streets, squares, parks and enclaves.

Modern London is the product of continual upheaval. When Queen Boudicca razed the original Roman city (built in AD 61), it was just the first of its many setbacks. The plague of 1665 claimed the lives of over 110,000 Londoners, and in 1666 the Great Fire that began in Pudding Lane destroyed much of the city. In the bombing blitz of World War II, 29,000 Londoners were killed, 80 percent of buildings in the City (the financial district) were damaged and a third were destroyed.

Yet each destruction bore its own seeds of change. The bombing of World War II eventually provided the opportunity for widening and lightening; slums disappeared, street crime and disease declined, and a crop of modern buildings were constructed.

A CITY IN VOGUE

Every now and then the city becomes brazenly fashionable – from the Swinging London of the 1960s, or 'the coolest place on the planet', as *Newsweek* dubbed it in the 1990s, through to the punk phenomenon of the 70s, the glam, high camp 80s to the grungy 90s

WHEN TO GO

London can be busy all year round, and it's impossible to plan based on England's famously treacherous and unpredictable weather. High season is throughout the summer (June–Aug), when tourism peaks, attractions are busier and prices for accommodation skyrocket – but these months offer the best chance of sunshine and are ideal for enjoying the capital's outdoor markets and beautiful green spaces. London can be less expensive, with fewer crowds, in the shoulder months of spring (March–May), when flowers are in bloom and events such as the boat race and the London Marathon take place, and autumn (Sept–Nov), when crisp, clear sunshine adorns the skies, and the city is buzzing with fashion week and film and literature festivals. December is also a high season – it's one of the most exciting times to visit, when you can enjoy the Christmas markets and festivities, and cosy pubs with heated outdoor areas. There's no true low season but the quietest and cheapest (though most dreary) months tend to be January and February, but this is a great time for shopping in the New Year sales.

and 00s, through to a fusion of styles in recent decades. London has long held its status as one of the fashion capitals of the world. And style has always had a soundtrack to match – from the jazz of the 1950s through to explosive 60s rock, to waves of pop, house, electronic, indie and grime. London's musical heritage is ever-present

SUSTAINABLE TRAVEL

You might not realise at first, but over a third of this sprawling city is green space. In 2019 London became the world's first ever **National Park City**, an honour which celebrates the city's abundant parks and wildlife areas and aims to protect and improve its green credentials in future. Whether you're cycling in Richmond Park or exploring the famous botanical gardens in Kew, picnicking in Hyde Park or taking in the stunning views at Greenwich Park, boating in Battersea Park or swimming in the ponds of Hampstead Heath, there's plenty to do in these beautiful green spaces for a sustainable day out.

London now boasts four restaurants with **Michelin Green Stars**, a culinary accolade for exceptional sustainable practices, including *Petersham Nurseries Café* in Richmond, *St. Barts* in the City, *Apricity* in Mayfair and *Silo*, the world's first **zero-waste restaurant** which opened in Hackney Wick in 2019 (see page 131).

In 2023, to help keep emissions down, the city expanded its **Ultra Low Emission Zone (ULEZ)** to all boroughs across London, issuing a charge for vehicles that don't comply with emissions standards. London's tubes, trains and buses offer much better (and quicker) ways to get around, and you likely won't turn a corner without seeing one of the many **bicycles for hire** dotted across the city.

As one of the world's leading sustainable cities, it can be said that London has come some way since it earned the name the 'Big Smoke', but there is a long way to go. Recent years have seen increasingly more environmental protests across the city, bringing awareness to climate issues and demonstrating against detrimental government policies. For ways to make your visit to London more sustainable, see the **Sustainability Pledge** on the **Visit London** website (www.visitlondon.com), the city's official tourism website.

in its streets, bars and clubs, eternally connecting neighbourhoods.

A CITY OF SURPRISES

London is an ever-evolving patchwork of areas to explore, where you never know what you're going to find around the next corner. You might stumble on the pomp of State occasions, the grind of a weekend carnival, the buzz of an undiscovered eatery, the press of a narrow medieval alley, the surprise of a famous home or the serenity of a secret garden.

The Sky Garden

As the eighteenth-century English poet and playwright Samuel Johnson declared, 'when a man is tired of London, he is tired of life.'

LONDON CABBIES

Perhaps the closest most visitors get to meeting a true Londoner is when they catch a black cab. Taxi drivers, or cabbies, are experts on the city and are essential to its life, and about 17,000 work in London. The classic cab, the Austin FX4, was launched in 1958 and is still going strong in its updated incarnation. Prospective black cab drivers spend up to four years studying London's roads, remembering a total of 320 routes, as well as 25,000 streets and 20,000 places of interest. After passing a written exam and oral tests, drivers get their licence. You can trust that they always know where they're going.

10 Things not to miss

1 TOWER OF LONDON
Where many a historic head has rolled. See page 77.

2 HARRODS
London's most famous department store, known for its exquisite Art Nouveau food hall. See page 85.

3 TATE MODERN
Feted for its architecture and its excellent collection of modern and contemporary art. See page 64.

4 BIG BEN
The clocktower (officially renamed the Queen Elizabeth Tower) dominates the Palace of Westminster, home of the Parliament. See page 39.

5 NATIONAL GALLERY
Located in Trafalgar Square, it houses Britain's finest collection of European art. See page 34.

6 THE BRITISH MUSEUM
Situated in Bloomsbury, it houses artefacts from antiquity to the present. See page 55.

7 COVENT GARDEN
Named after its market, it's a lively area for shopping and street performance. See page 45.

8 ST PAUL'S CATHEDRAL
Sir Christopher Wren's masterpiece is the jewel of the City. See page 73.

9 BUCKINGHAM PALACE
Witness age-old traditions at the King's London residence. See page 50.

10 THE LONDON EYE
Take a ride for spectacular views over London. See page 62.

A perfect day in London

9.30AM
Breakfast. Get the day off to a good start with a full English breakfast from the superb breakfast menu at *The Wolseley* on Piccadilly.

10AM
Royal Park. Take a morning stroll in one of London's leafy central parks – St James's, Green or Hyde. Catch the Changing of the Guard on the hour from 11am Mon–Sat (10am Sun) at Horse Guards Parade or at 11am at Buckingham Palace (only every other day Aug–Apr).

NOON
Culture fix. Take the Piccadilly line to Russell Square and walk to the British Museum, a treasure trove of world artefacts. Among the highlights are the Elgin Marbles and the stunning Egyptian collection. If you're hungry, grab a snack at the café in the magnificent Great Court.

2PM
Covent Garden. Head south via Seven Dials towards Covent Garden, where retail therapy options abound. Meander along Neal Street, lined with fashion-forward boutiques, to Long Acre, where upmarket chain stores offer a more high-street experience.

3.30PM
Art and cake. Ten minutes' walk away is the National Portrait Gallery, where you can check out some famous portraits, from royals throughout the centuries to artists in their studios, then settle into the rooftop restaurant, *The Portrait*, with its spectacular views of Westminster, for a traditional afternoon tea.

5PM
Westminster. Take a walk through Trafalgar Square and south along Whitehall to Parliament Square, where you will find Westminster Abbey, the Houses of Parliament and Big Ben. Then head across the Thames on Westminster Bridge to the South Bank.

6.30PM
Southbank sunset. Just north of Westminster Bridge is the London Eye, a great way to get a bird's eye view of London at sunset, or the city lights at night. If you're ready for another rest stop, atmospheric *Gordon's Wine Bar* (see page 122), the oldest in London, is just across the Hungerford Bridge and Golden Jubilee Bridges at 47 Villiers Street.

8.30PM
East End dining. Get the District line from Embankment to Aldgate East, a short walk from vibrant Brick Lane. Try Tayyabs (see page 132) on nearby Fieldgate Street for affordable, authentic Punjabi cuisine. Alternatively, get off at Cannon Street, walk past St Paul's Cathedral and enjoy great views as you have a drink or dine at Madison on the rooftop of the One New Change shopping centre.

The best of London Bridge

9AM

Tower of London. Avoid the crowds and head to Tower Hill bright and early to visit the historic Tower of London. Either grab breakfast on the way, or head to *Café Rouge* at St Katherine's Docks (www.caferouge.com; 6min walk from Tower Hill station) for breakfast with views of the marina. When you're ready, learn all about the Bloody Tower's infamous history as a prison, view the crown jewels and meet the legendary guardians of the tower – the ravens.

12PM

Tower Bridge. Walk over London's iconic Tower Bridge, which is also the UK's most recognisable bridge (have your camera at the ready). There's also a museum inside this famous landmark (see page 70), where you can explore the engine rooms and walk across the high-level glass floors for spectacular views of the structure and of the Thames. Afterwards, once over the bridge, turn right onto the riverside path and head to Borough Market.

12.30PM

Market lunch. Lunch at Borough Market. Spend some time getting the lay of the land and working out which stalls are where. You'll find some of the most delicious market food here at this vibrant spot, from Indian to Spanish, Lebanese, Korean and more, and some of London's best restaurants have outposts here. It's sometimes heaving, especially on weekends, but keep a calm head, find somewhere to perch and enjoy the atmosphere!

3PM

Modern art. After lunch, wander through the lively streets and back along the river towards the Tate Modern (see page 64). Try to get here for around 3pm for at least a couple of hours viewing time (the building itself is stunning and worth exploration, including the great Turbine Hall and the tenth-floor viewing gallery). This is the best museum for art from the 1900s onwards and has hosted landmark exhibitions on everyone from Picasso and Kandinsky to Dorothea Tanning, Yayoi Kusama and Lubaina Himid.

6PM

Historic walks. Head back towards the Borough Market area, winding your way through the interesting medieval streets. You might want to pass via the atmospheric ruins of Winchester Palace on Pickford's Wharf, or wander around the recently developed Borough Yards under the area's historic railway arches.

7PM

Dinnertime. Find a bar or pub to pitch up in and get in the 'virtual queue' for *Padella* (see page 128) – Londoners' favourite pasta bar. Once you're in, sit on the high stools in front of the kitchen area and watch the pasta chefs work their magic, or grab a cosy table in the ambient downstairs.

A day out around Greenwich

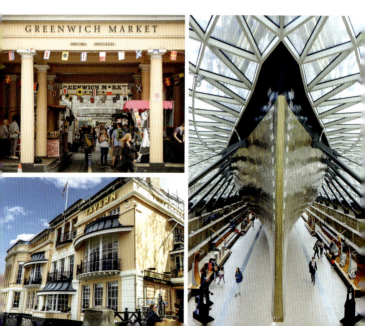

9AM

Breakfast. Start the day in the picturesque village of Blackheath, which sits just north of Greenwich Park. Enjoy coffee and fresh pastries at *GAIL's* bakery (3 Blackheath Village), then wander up and down the charming high street, lined with shops, cafés and restaurants.

10AM

Morning ramble. Walk up the hill towards the heath and along Tranquil Vale. You'll see the All Saints' Church across the heath on your right, some pretty Georgian houses on your left, then a bit further along you'll reach the Hare and Billett pub and pond – take a right at this roundabout and walk toward the Millenium Circle on the heath. A bit further along you'll reach Charlton Way and the entrance to Greenwich Park. The park itself is lovely to walk around, but if you walk straight along the main road from the entrance (Blackheath Avenue) you'll reach the Royal Observatory, where you can see the Meridian Line and one of the UK's largest telescopes (see page 95). Outside, take in the fantastic views from the top of the hill, then follow the path down to the left towards the National Maritime Museum.

1PM

Local history. The Maritime Museum (its entrance is marked by the large ship in a bottle) deserves a couple of hours to explore the excellent galleries and photography displays (see page 95). If you're hungry, pick up a snack at the museum's *Parkside Café*.

3PM

Pie and mash. When you leave the museum, head down to *Goddards at Greenwich* on (22 King William Walk; www.goddardsatgreenwich.co.uk) for a late lunch (see page 118). This traditional pie and mash shop has been here since the 1800s and is steeped in history.

5PM

Greenwich highlights. Once you've had your fill, spend the afternoon wandering around Greenwich. Further down King William Walk is Greenwich Market, full of art and antiques stalls (there's also a vintage market, Fri–Sun only). Another highlight in Greenwich is the staggering *Cutty Sark*, a nineteenth-century ship, now permanently docked near the river and housing a museum (see page 95).

6PM

Evening drinks. If you haven't noticed by now, Greenwich is full to the brim of cosy pubs, so spend your evening sampling some of southeast London's finest. A few worth visiting are *The Gipsy Moth* (www.thegipsymothgreenwich.co.uk), just by Cutty Sark, which has a great atmosphere and large beer garden, the characterful riverside *Trafalgar Tavern* (www.trafalgartavern.co.uk), or the Old Brewery, housed inside the Old Royal Naval College (www.oldbrewerygreenwich.com).

History

Although Julius Caesar landed in England in 56 and 55 BC, he came, he saw and he left without leaving any trace of a settlement. It remained for the Emperor Claudius and his Roman legions to conquer the island in AD 43 and build what was believed to be the first bridge over the Thames – roughly on the site of today's London Bridge – establishing the trade port of Londinium.

The Romans built roads, forts, temples, villas, a basilica, forum and a huge amphitheatre (excavated near the Guildhall in 1988) for a population of around 50,000 living in the area now known as the City. The Roman's rule was often challenged, and so they erected vast stone walls around their city.

SAXONS AND NORMANS

In 410, as the Roman Empire declined, London's legions were recalled to Rome. The walled area of Londinium became a ghost town, buried under silt and grass, and avoided by subsequent invaders. Eventually, the Saxons came over the North Sea to build Lundenwic, and, after a brief return to paganism, the seeds of Christianity – sown in the later-Roman period – sprouted in London again. St Ethelbert, the first Christian king, dedicated a small church to St Paul here; it has since been destroyed and rebuilt five times.

The Saxon kings were constantly at battle with Viking and Danish invaders, and when the Danes conquered and put King Canute on the throne in 1016, London unseated Winchester as the capital of the kingdom. In the 1040s Westminster Abbey was built by Edward the Confessor, a pious though ineffectual king. When the Norman army of William the Conqueror was victorious at the Battle of Hastings in 1066, William began the tradition of being crowned at the Abbey. He respected London's wealth and commercial energy, and shrewdly forged a relationship with the Church and citizenry that benefited all concerned. He also instigated work on the Tower of London.

FEUDAL ENGLAND

During the early Middle Ages London's influence grew, while the kings of England were diverted by wars in France and Crusades to the Holy Land. Under Henry I, London's citizens won the right to choose their own magistrates, and during the reign of the absentee king, Richard the Lionheart (1189–1199), the elective office of Mayor (later Lord Mayor) was created.

The Tower of London

England's medieval monarchs did not enjoy blind loyalty from London's citizens, whose strong trade and craft guilds, which still exist, created a self-determinism and power that often resulted in rebellions. The Palace of Westminster became the seat of government, and one of the reputed reasons for its riverside site was that a mob could not surround it.

By 1340 London's population hit around 50,000, but in 1348 disaster struck. The Black Death swept across Eurasia, killing 75 million. Details of the horrors in London are scarce, and there are no accurate figures on the final death toll; however, it is estimated that almost half of London's population was hit.

London was still little bigger than it had been in Roman times, but this was about to change. The decision by Henry VIII to break

Portrait of Elizabeth I

relations with Rome gave birth to the Church of England and also added property in the form of seized monastery lands, such as Covent Garden (once a convent garden).

THE ELIZABETHAN ERA

Between the death of Henry VIII in 1547 and the coronation of his daughter Elizabeth I in 1558, religious persecutions and political intrigues drained the kingdom's coffers and influence. However, under the 45-year reign of Elizabeth, England rose to unforeseen heights, with London the epicentre of a mighty kingdom. The defeat of the Spanish Armada in 1588 signalled the dawn of empire, as the British Navy took to the seas in search of riches. The prosperity of Elizabeth's reign was marked by the blossoming of English literature, with Shakespeare the jewel in the crown of literati including Christopher Marlowe and Ben Jonson.

REVOLUTION AND RESTORATION

In marked contrast, Elizabeth's successors are remembered principally for their failures. In 1605 James I narrowly escaped assassination in the abortive Gunpowder Plot – Guy Fawkes was discovered in the cellars of the Houses of Parliament about to light the fuse that would have blown up the king at the opening of Parliament on November 5. This act is still commemorated annually around the country on 'Bonfire Night'.

James I's son, Charles I, was even less popular. By attempting to dissolve Parliament, the feckless king plunged the country into Civil War. In 1642 the Royalists ('Cavaliers'), supported by the aristocracy, went into battle against the Parliamentary forces. The 'Roundheads', named after their 'pudding-basin' hairstyle, were backed by the tradesmen and Puritans, and led by Oliver Cromwell. The Royalists were defeated at Naseby, Northamptonshire, in 1645. In 1649 Charles I was found guilty of treason and beheaded. Cromwell assumed power and abolished the monarchy, and for a short period Britain was a republic. In 1653 Cromwell declared himself Lord Protector, remaining so until his death in 1658. However, by 1660 the country was disenchanted with the dreary dictatorship of Puritan rule, and the monarchy was restored under Charles II.

DISASTERS AND RECOVERY

In 1665 a terrible plague stalked London, killing an estimated 110,000 people. Death, disease and decay soon devastated the city, in which piles of bodies were left in its streets.

In 1666 disaster struck again, in the form of the Great Fire. About 80 percent of the old City burnt down, and 100,000 people were made homeless. Incredibly, due to a speedy evacuation, the number of recorded deaths is in single figures. Sir Christopher Wren was appointed joint head of a commission to oversee the rebuilding of the city, and though his grand schemes were never fully realised, he made a huge contribution to the new London, including rebuilding St Paul's. The Monument (see page 77) is his memorial to the fire.

The final great confrontation between king and parliament involved James II, brother of Charles II. A fervent Catholic, James attacked the Church of England and disregarded the laws of the land. However, the people of England had no stomach for cutting

Stained glass portrait of Dr Samuel Johnson, Fleet Street

off another royal head, and in 1688 James fled the country. The so-called Glorious (peaceful) Revolution ushered in William of Orange and Mary II to the throne, establishing a stable constitutional monarchy. Under William and Mary, a royal retreat was established at Kensington Palace.

GEORGIAN GREATNESS

In the eighteenth and early nineteenth centuries, London was the capital of a world power. In the coffeehouses of the City and West End, poets and men of letters such as Alexander Pope and Samuel Johnson were prominent cultural figures. Handel was court composer to King George I, and Kew Gardens and the British Museum were opened to the public. But there was a dark side to London – slums grew up south of the river and in the East End, and crime was rife.

Overseas the Empire was burgeoning, until a tax dispute caused a rift between Britain and the American colonies. This escalated into a war over independence, and, to the astonishment of George III, the colonists won. By the end of the eighteenth century, Britain was threatened with Napoleonic invasion, but Nelson disposed of the French fleet at the Battle of Trafalgar in 1805. Some 10 years later, the Duke of Wellington put an end to Napoleon's ambitions at the Battle of Waterloo.

THE VICTORIAN EMPIRE

The accession of the 18-year-old Queen Victoria in 1837 gave title to England's most expansive age. The Empire building that was started in Elizabeth I's day was taken to new heights in the nineteenth century. Ships filled with the bounty of the colonies not only brought goods with which to trade at the East End docks, they also drew in new languages, cultures and citizens who helped to shape the cosmopolitan capital.

In 1851 Victorian progress was feted at the Great Exhibition, held in Hyde Park in Joseph Paxton's vast, specially designed iron-and-glass Crystal Palace. Transported south of the Thames to Sydenham in 1852, the edifice gave its name to a new Victorian suburb, Crystal Palace; sadly, the grandiose building itself burned down in 1936.

With the money taken at the Great Exhibition, Prince Albert, Queen Victoria's consort, realised his ambition: a centre of learning in the form of the Victoria and Albert Museum. This was followed by the Queen's tributes to her husband, the Royal Albert Hall and Royal Albert Memorial.

However, while the rich grew fat and complacent, the poor were increasingly wretched, and the pen of Charles Dickens pricked

BLUE PLAQUES

In 1867 the first blue ceramic plaque was erected on the front of 24 Holles Street by the Royal Society of Arts (RA) to commemorate Lord Byron, who was born there. Across London there are now over 1000 such plaques, each linking famous figures with the buildings they were associated with. The range has so far been dominated by politicians and artists – and males, who account for 85 percent of plaques. Since 2016, English Heritage has been committed to tackling this disparity. In 2024 new plaques were unveiled for more women including Diana Beck (in Marylebone), the UK's first female neurosurgeon, and jazz singer and BBC broadcaster Adelaide Hall (in Kensington).

many a middle-class conscience with his portrayal of the misery and hopelessness of the souls condemned to poverty in this 'prosperous' city. London was growing rapidly, and by 1861 it had 3 million inhabitants. The East End slums expanded to house the newcomers pouring into the city looking for work. The boundaries of London were pushed well out into the countryside with the development of public transport. Newly invented omnibuses, trains and, in 1863, the world's first underground railway, created a new breed of London citizen; the commuter.

TWO WORLD WARS

In 1915 the German Zeppelins dropped the first bombs on London, and World War I left London's young generation grossly depleted. This was a mere foretaste of what was to come 25 years later – Hitler's Blitzkrieg rained bombs down on London between September 1940 and May 1941, during which the city experienced 57 consecutive nights of bombing. In June 1944 the rockets known as 'doodlebugs' were launched, battering London until March 1945. By the end of the war London's death toll was over 30,000, with 3.5 million homes damaged or destroyed. Through it all strode Winston Churchill, the indomitable spirit of wartime Britain.

POST-WAR BOOM

Life in post-war Britain was spent clearing rubble and living frugally. By the 1950s, however, spirits were lifting, and, 100 years after the success of the Great Exhibition, the arts were feted again in the capital in 1951 at the Festival of Britain. The greatest legacy of the festival was the South Bank Centre, an arts complex built south of the Thames. London enjoyed a huge boom of popularity into the 1960s, when a stream of rock and rollers, artists and fashion designers put London firmly on the map. The explosion of anarchic punk culture in the 1970s was followed by the rampant materialism of Thatcherism and Conservative rule from 1979 to 1997.

LABOUR'S LEGACY

Most Londoners welcomed Labour's landslide victory in the 1997 election under Tony Blair. As areas of the city including Bankside were regenerated and London creatives dominated the arts, the British capital was celebrated in the press as 'the coolest place on the planet'. The millennium saw more successful developments, including the London Eye and Tate Modern. Labour decided to restore a measure of self-government to the capital by creating an elected

Scene on the Thames during the Blitz, 1940

mayor. Changes introduced by the first mayor, Ken Livingstone, included the 'congestion charge' aimed at tackling traffic jams and pollution.

By 2005, Labour's ongoing popularity had slipped significantly, thanks in no small part to Blair's controversial decision to go to war in Iraq. On July 7, 2005, London suffered a severe blow when, in Britain's first suicide-bombing, terrorists hit Underground and bus targets in the capital, killing 52 people and injuring around 700.

CONSERVATISM, AUSTERITY MEASURES AND BREXIT

In the 2010 general election, Labour – by then led by Gordon Brown – was defeated; the new government was a Conservative/

Liberal Democrat coalition, who introduced a programme of austerity measures to tackle the national deficit.

In 2011 the wedding of Prince William to Catherine (Kate) Middleton lifted spirits. This was followed, in 2012, by Queen Elizabeth II's Diamond Jubilee and the Olympic and Paralympic Games, which boosted the UK economy by £9.9 billion, and the following year saw more economic and tourist growth in London.. In April 2015, David Cameron led the Conservative Party to victory in the general election. In June 2016, he called for a referendum on Britain's membership of the European Union, bringing long-simmering concerns over British sovereignty and immigration to the fore. The UK narrowly voted to leave ('Brexit'), although London bucked the national trend with 59.9 percent opting to remain. Cameron immediately resigned, and Theresa May became Britain's second female prime minister in July.

Countdown to the Olympic Games

On March 22, 2017, a terrorist drove into pedestrians on Westminster Bridge, killing four, before fatally stabbing a policeman outside the Houses of Parliament. Only a couple of months later, on June 3, terrorists killed eight and injured 48 at Borough Market. In between the shocking attacks, May triggered Article 50, the two-year negotiation period for agreeing a divorce settlement with the EU. In June, a fire broke out Grenfell Tower, a high-rise block of residential flats in West London, killing 72 residents. The devastating event led to a six-year enquiry into government and construction failures, also highlighting housing inequality across London.

In May 2018, Prince Harry and Meghan Markle got married at a star-studded event in Windsor Castle. In January 2020, after continual media intrusion and reported rifts within the royal family, they stepped down from royal duties. In the same month, on January 31, the UK officially withdrew from the EU.

CLIMATE CONCERNS, THE COVID YEARS AND NEW RULE

In October 2018, Extinction Rebellion, a grassroots environmental group, staged protests around parliament and blocked five bridges across the city, causing major disruptions while urging the government to acknowledge the climate crisis. In April 2019, thousands again occupied the streets and over a thousand people were arrested. Later that year, Boris Johnson became prime minister, succeeding Theresa May.

In March 2020, following the global outbreak of coronavirus, the UK went into lockdown. Government-imposed restrictions continued for two years to tackle the pandemic, including travel bans, event cancellations, and mass closures across the country. Just a couple of months later, following the murder of George Floyd in the US by a police officer, people took to London's streets for a major Black Lives Matter demonstration against systemic racism. Protests continued throughout the year.

On September 8, 2022, Queen Elizabeth II died aged 96, having reigned for 70 years and 214 days – Britain's longest-reigning monarch. Her funeral was held on September 19 at Westminster Abbey and processions were held throughout London, with over a million people lining the streets. She was buried with her husband, Prince Philip, who died in 2021, and succeeded by her son, King Charles

Flowers for Queen Elizabeth

III, whose official coronation was held in 2023.

Boris Johnson resigned as prime minister in September 2022 and was succeeded by Liz Truss, who held office for 45 days. Rishi Sunak then became prime minister in October. In 2024, after years of increasing dissatisfaction with Conservative leadership, the Labour Party won the general election with a historic landslide. Keir Starmer became prime minister.

CHRONOLOGY

AD 43 Emperor Claudius establishes the trade port of Londinium.
61 Boudicca sacks the city but is defeated, and London is rebuilt.
c.200 City wall built. London becomes the capital of Britannia Superior.
410 Romans withdraw to defend Rome. London falls into decline.
884 London becomes the capital under Alfred the Great.
1348–9 Black Death wipes out 50 percent of London's population.
1534 Henry VIII declares himself head of the Church of England.
1605 Guy Fawkes attempts to blow up James I and Parliament.
1642–9 Civil war between Royalists and Roundheads.
1665 Plague hits London again, killing around 110,000 citizens.
1666 Great Fire of London.
1837–1901 Victorian Empire-building and the Industrial Revolution.

CHRONOLOGY

1851 Great Exhibition in Joseph Paxton's Crystal Palace in Hyde Park.
1863 London Underground opens its first line, the Metropolitan line.
1888 Serial murderer Jack the Ripper strikes in Whitechapel.
1914–18 World War I. Zeppelins bomb London.
1922 The BBC transmits its first radio programmes.
1939–45 World War II. London is heavily bombed.
1951 Festival of Britain. South Bank Centre built adjacent to Waterloo.
1980s Margaret Thatcher years. Several IRA bombs hit London.
1996 Shakespeare's Globe opens on Bankside.
2000 London celebrates the millennium. Ken Livingstone elected Mayor.
2005 Suicide bombers kill 52 and injure approximately 700 people.
2008 Boris Johnson elected Mayor of London. Global Financial Crisis.
2012 Queen's Jubilee. Olympics held in London. Johnson re-elected.
2013 The Duchess of Cambridge gives birth to Prince George. Princess Charlotte follows in 2015, Prince Louis in 2018.
2015 The Conservative Party win the general election.
2016 Sadiq Khan is elected Mayor of London. The UK narrowly votes leave in EU referendum.
2017 Five people killed in Westminster terrorist attack. UK triggers Article 50. Eight die in Borough Market terror attack. Fire breaks out at Grenfell Tower, killing 72.
2018 Prince Harry and Meghan Markle get married.
2020 The UK leaves the EU on January 31. In March, the country goes into national lockdown due to the Covid-19 pandemic. Restrictions continue for the next two years.
2022 Queen Elizabeth dies aged 96, succeeded by King Charles III who is officially crowned in 2023.
2024 The Labour Party win the general election, Keir Starmer becomes prime minister.

Big Ben and Westminster Bridge

Places

There are as many opinions on the best way to tour London as there are places to see. First-time visitors may find a ride on an open-top bus (see page 142) helpful in getting their bearings round the city centre. Once you've identified which area to explore, it's best to pound the streets, and seeing London this way enables you to trace the city's development through its varied architecture.

WESTMINSTER

HIGHLIGHTS

- » Trafalgar Square, see page 33
- » Whitehall, see page 36
- » The Houses of Parliament, see page 38
- » Westminster Abbey, see page 39
- » Tate Britain, see page 51

The centre of official London, Westminster today is very different from its eleventh-century origins as a marshy island where Edward the Confessor built a church, 'West Minster', and a palace. Nowadays, it is home to the UK Parliament and London's *grand place*, Trafalgar Square.

TRAFALGAR SQUARE

Named after the naval battle that took place in 1805 off Cape Trafalgar, southwest Spain – at which Admiral Lord Nelson defeated Napoleon – **Trafalgar Square** ❶ is as good a place as any to start a tour of London. Once criticised as little more than a glorified, polluted roundabout, the north side has been completely pedestrianised and the square has become the focus for many of London's top cultural events, celebrations, festivals and political protests.

Trafalgar Square and Nelson's Column

Towering high above the square is the 170ft (52-metre) **Nelson's Column**, topped by a statue of Britain's most famous maritime hero. Adjacent are the stone lions by Sir Edwin Landseer that provide a popular spot for tourists after photo opportunities. Look out for the fourth plinth, in the northwest corner of the square, used to showcase temporary works of art by contemporary artists – from a giant whipped cream sculpture by Heather Phillipson to a thought-provoking memorial to transgender victims of violence by Teresa Margolles. Past commissions have gone to Antony Gormley, Rachel Whiteread, Marc Quinn and David Shrigley.

National Gallery

Dominating the north side of the square is the **National Gallery** (www.nationalgallery.org.uk; free except some special exhibitions), which houses Britain's finest collection of European art dating from 1250 to 1900. The gallery was founded in 1824, when a private collection of 38 paintings was acquired by the British Government for £57,000 and exhibited in the owner's house at 100 Pall Mall. As the collection grew, a new building to accommodate it was planned. William Wilkins' grand neoclassical building opened in 1838 in the then-recently created Trafalgar Square. The Sainsbury Wing, to the west of Wilkins' building, was added in 1991, designed by the American architect Robert Venturi in witty postmodern style. The two buildings are bridged by a circular link, and the pleasant paved area between them offers a short-cut to Leicester Square (see page 45).

The collection, which contains over two thousand works, is divided into four sections. The Sainsbury Wing (temporarily closed until 2025, check website for artworks relocated to other rooms) usually houses paintings from 1250 to 1500, including Jan van Eyck's *Arnolfini Portrait* and Leonardo da Vinci's *The Virgin of the Rocks*. The West Wing contains paintings from 1500 to 1600, including Titian's *Bacchus and Ariadne* and Holbein the Younger's *The Ambassadors*. In the North Wing you can admire paintings from 1600 to 1700 including Velázquez's *Rokeby Venus* (which often finds itself at the centre of political protests), Rembrandt's *Self Portrait*, and Van Dyck's *Equestrian Portrait of Charles I*. The East Wing covers art from 1700 to early twentieth century and includes works by the English painters Constable and Gainsborough and Impressionists such as Monet, Van Gogh, Cézanne and Renoir.

National Portrait Gallery

Adjoining the National Gallery, the **National Portrait Gallery** (2 St Martin's Place; www.npg.org.uk; free except special exhibitions) was founded in 1856 as a 'Gallery of the Portraits of the most eminent persons in British History'. Additions to the collection have always been determined by the status of the sitter and historical importance of the portrait, not by their quality as works of art. Highlights include Holbein's drawing of Henry VII and his son Henry VIII, a life-like portrait of Queen Elizabeth I, in brocade and pearls, and self-portraits of Hogarth, Gainsborough and Reynolds.

St-Martin-in-the-Fields

At the northeast corner of the square is the church of **St Martin-in-the-Fields** (www.stmartin-in-the-fields.org; free). This is the oldest

WHERE TO SHOOT THE BEST PICTURES

The **Buckingham Palace Gardens** offer a unique opportunity to picnic on the lawns with views of the palace. You can get a great shot of **St Paul's** from the Millennium Bridge, which presents quite the photo opportunity. Get up early and get a perfect snap of the lions and sculptures at **Trafalgar Square** before the crowds descend. Level 72 is the highest spot at **The Shard** and has excellent views over the city. There's a great view of the **London Eye** from Westminster Bridge, or ride the wheel itself to see other landmarks from the air. The famous Abbey Road zebra crossing is outside **Abbey Road Studios** near St John's Wood station (Northern Line) and is an iconic photograph that tourists love to replicate. Head to St Katherine Docks or London Bridge to get a stunning shot of **Tower Bridge** in all its glory. Finally, in **Richmond Park**, which can look quite spectacular in spring or autumn, there are plenty of wildlife spotting opportunities; the Isabella Plantation (home to over 60 species of birds) is a particularly good location. Generally, sunrise or sunset are wonderful times to take photos around London – the colours are often prettiest, the light softest, and you'll avoid the usual crowds.

building in Trafalgar Square, built in 1724 by a Scottish architect, James Gibbs, when the venue was literally in fields outside the city. This is the parish church of the royal family and the royal box can be seen on the left of the altar. Nell Gwynne, mistress of Charles II, is one of several famous people buried here. The church is renowned for its classical and jazz concerts, held at lunchtimes and in the evenings. The atmospheric crypt houses a brass-rubbing centre and a pleasant café.

WHITEHALL

The avenue of government buildings that runs south from Trafalgar Square to Parliament Square is named after Henry VIII's Palace of Whitehall, which once stood on this spot, but burned

WHITEHALL 37

down in 1698. The first major place of interest on the west side of the street is the Palladian-style **Horse Guards** ❷, built between 1751–3 on the site where the main gateway to the Palace of Whitehall once stood. Two mounted Life Guards duly maintain their traditional sentry posts between 10am and 4pm each day, changing every hour (www.royal.gov.uk). The archway in the building leads through to the huge Horse Guards Parade ground, which adjoins St James's Park (see page 142).

Opposite Horse Guards is **Banqueting House** (www.hrp.org.uk; closed for maintenance, expected to reopen in 2025), one of England's first Renaissance buildings, and the only surviving part of the Palace of Whitehall. It was built in 1619 by Inigo Jones for James I and inspired by Jones's hero, the sixteenth-century Italian master Palladio. Its major interior feature is a splendid ceiling by Rubens, commissioned by Charles I. Ironically, Charles was later beheaded in front of this very building.

A little further down on the right hand side is **10 Downing Street** (www.gov.uk/government/organisations/prime-ministers-office-10-downing-street), office and residence of the prime minister since 1735. Barriers at the end of the street prevent the public from viewing the famous doorway.

Just south of here in the middle of the street is the **Cenotaph**, a memorial

King's Life Guard

Henry VII Chapel inside Westminster Abbey

designed by Sir Edwyn Lutyens commemorating the dead of both world wars. Continuing south towards Parliament Square you pass the imposing headquarters of the Foreign Office and the Treasury. At the far end of King Charles Street, which runs between them, are the **Churchill War Rooms** (www.iwm.org.uk; charge), where you can explore Churchill's underground World War II command post and a museum about his life and work.

THE HOUSES OF PARLIAMENT

The neo-Gothic Victorian triumph on the banks of the Thames is the **Palace of Westminster** ❸, better known as the Houses of Parliament. Guided tours (90 mins; charge) are available on Saturdays throughout the year and Tues–Sat during the summer recess (www.parliament.uk). At other times of year, UK residents can contact their MP to request a free tour (75 mins) or free tickets to watch a parliamentary debate (Prime Minister's Question Time is on Wednesdays from noon) and overseas residents can obtain tickets for debates by queuing on the day.

The original palace was built for Edward the Confessor around 1065, and for four hundred years it was a royal residence. However, the only medieval part of the palace remaining is Westminster Hall, built in 1099. In 1834, someone disposed of several ancient wooden tally-rods in the basement furnace, and the resulting conflagration consumed most of the building. Many considered it a blessing to be able to rebuild the draughty old edifice. The architect Sir Charles Barry was the driving force behind the new design, a 'great and beautiful monument to Victorian artifice', which was completed in 1860.

The most famous element of Barry's design is the clock tower housing **Big Ben** (UK residents can arrange a free tour by contacting their MP; no children under 11), a 13.5-ton bell, officially renamed the Elizabeth Tower in 2012, in honour of Queen Elizabeth II's 60-year reign. Its popular name is thought to commemorate Sir Benjamin Hall, Chief Commissioner of Works when the bell was cast in 1859; however, it may also have been named after a boxer of the day, Benjamin Caunt.

WESTMINSTER ABBEY

Facing the Houses of Parliament is **Westminster Abbey** ❹ (www.westminster-abbey.org). Henry III built much of the abbey in the thirteenth century in early English Gothic-style, and it remained an important monastery until

— **NOTES** —

Literary figures buried in Poets' Corner include Alfred Tennyson, Ben Jonson (who is buried standing upright), Thomas Hardy, Charles Dickens and Rudyard Kipling. Others commemorated here include Jane Austen, the Brontë sisters and, more recently, Ted Hughes.

> **NOTES**
>
> If you're interested in visiting both Tate galleries, the Tate Boat runs all year round between Tate Britain and Tate Modern during gallery opening hours, and also stops at the Embankment, near Westminster. Ticket information can be found here www.tate.org.uk/visit/tate-boat.

1534 when Henry VIII dissolved the monasteries. After this, the abbey was still used as the royal church for coronations and burials, and all but two monarchs since William the Conqueror have been crowned here. The last coronation was held here on May 6, 2023, for King Charles III.

Beyond the nave, in the south transept, is **Poets' Corner**. Geoffrey Chaucer was the first poet to be buried here, in 1400. Behind the sanctuary are ornate royal chapels and tombs. The **Tomb of the Unknown Warrior**, west of the nave, holds the body of a soldier brought from France after World War I.

In 2018, the abbey's medieval galleries, located 70ft (21m) above the nave, opened for the first time in seven hundred years. The Queen's Diamond Jubilee Galleries (charge) displays a collection of treasures, along with excellent views into the church and across Parliament Square.

Southwest of here, at the other end of Victoria Street, is London's Roman Catholic cathedral, the outlandish Italian-Byzantine style **Westminster Cathedral** (www.westminstercathedral.org.uk; free), which dates from the nineteenth century. There are fine views from the Viewing Gallery, perched 210ft (64-metres) up its distinctive striped tower.

TATE BRITAIN

About 15 minutes' walk south of Parliament Square, on the riverside near Vauxhall Bridge, is **Tate Britain** ❺ (www.tate.org.uk; free except some special exhibitions). The nearest tube station is Pimlico, from where the gallery is well signed.

TATE BRITAIN

Although somewhat eclipsed by its newer sister gallery, Tate Modern (see page 142), Tate Britain is still the main national gallery for British art, showcasing works from the sixteenth century to the present day. Some highlights of the collection include Hogarth portraits, Constable's *Flatford Mill*, Millais's *Ophelia*, the pre-Raphaelite paintings of Dante Gabriel Rossetti, Francis Bacon's *Study of a Dog*, David Hockney's *Mr and Mrs Clark and Percy* and artworks by Lubaina Himid. Among the British 20th-century sculptors represented are Jacob Epstein, Barbara Hepworth, Henry Moore and Sarah Lucas.

The Clore Gallery (an extension of the main building) was built in the 1980s to hold the Tate's huge and magnificent J.M.W. Turner collection, which includes 300 oil paintings and over 30,000 other works by the Covent Garden-born artist.

Classical oil paintings in Tate Britain

THE WEST END

HIGHLIGHTS
- Piccadilly Circus, see page 42
- Oxford Street, see page 43
- Soho and Chinatown, see pages 44 and 45
- Leicester Square, see page 45
- Covent Garden, see page 45
- Somerset House, see page 48
- The Embankment, see page 49

Despite its misleading name, which reflects the fact that it is west of 'The City', the West End is actually London's central shopping and entertainment hub. It is a sprawling part of town, stretching from Oxford Street in the north, through Soho, Chinatown and Covent Garden, to the Thames-side Embankment in the south. Though the area doesn't boast a lot of traditional 'sights', it is thronged with tourists and locals, day and night, as it is home to the city's greatest concentration of shops, theatres, restaurants, bars and clubs.

PICCADILLY CIRCUS

At the heart of the West End is bustling **Piccadilly Circus** ❻, whose illuminated advertisements first appeared in 1890. Three years later, a memorial to the philanthropic Seventh Earl of Shaftesbury was erected in the circus, topped by a statue of a winged figure, popularly known as 'Eros', but actually a representation of Anteros, the Greek god of selfless love.

Running northwest out of Piccadilly Circus is **Regent Street**, designed by John Nash as a ceremonial route to link Carlton House, the long-demolished Prince Regent's residence at Piccadilly, with Regent's Park. Despite the Regency connections, the elegant shop fronts disguise how young the street actually is – much of it was built in the 1920s, over 100 years after Nash began work. The main section of Regent Street – between Piccadilly Circus and Oxford Circus – is notable for its massive shops, including Arts and Crafts flagship store, Liberty, and the seven-floored Hamleys, the largest toyshop in the world.

OXFORD STREET

Bordered by Marble Arch to the west and the crossroads with Tottenham Court Road to the east, **Oxford Street** ❼ is the busiest and most famous – although admittedly not the most glamorous – of London's shopping streets. The quality of shops vary wildly, from market stalls and discount stores selling Union Jack T-shirts, through branches of most of the major high-street chains, to top-class institutions such as Selfridges department store.

Named after the Earl of Oxford, who owned land north of here from the sixteenth century, the road was built as a main route out of the city and was intended to link the counties of Hampshire and Suffolk. From the 1760s it began to develop as an entertainment centre. The Pantheon (replaced by Marks & Spencer in 1937) housed fetes and concerts, and Jack Broughton's amphitheatre, on the corner of Hanwell Street and Oxford Street, was famed for its boxing bouts and tiger baiting. By the late nineteenth century, however,

Piccadilly Circus

the street was becoming established as a place for retail therapy. Furniture store Waring & Gillow opened in 1906, while the department stores Selfridges and Debenham and Freebody opened in 1909 and 1919 respectively.

A couple of excellent little galleries worth visiting around Oxford Street are **The Cartoon Museum** (63 Wells Street; www.cartoonmuseum.org; charge) and the **Photographers' Gallery** (16–18 Ramillies Street; www.thephotographersgallery.org.uk; charge).

SOHO AND CHINATOWN

Soho ❽, the area bordered by Regent Street, Oxford Street, Charing Cross Road and Shaftesbury Avenue, has long been the focal point of London's nightlife. Soho is characterised by narrow streets peppered with bars, cafés, restaurants, theatres, small shops and boutiques, though life has not always been so hectic here. Before the 1666 Great Fire of London, this area was open land where people came to hunt – the name 'Soho' is thought to derive from a hunting cry. After the fire, the area's open land was used for new housing and, in the late-seventeenth and eighteenth centuries, it was inhabited by noblemen and eminent socialites.

However, by the nineteenth century, wealthy Londoners were moving out to Mayfair (see page 53),

Chinatown

and Soho was taken over by the bohemian crowd. Its coffee houses and alehouses soon became places for debate, founding a tradition that continues today in drinking clubs such as the Groucho Club. In the twentieth century the area became increasingly cosmopolitan. By the 'swinging sixties', Soho's seedier side had come to the fore, and sex work and the porn industry were rife. In 1972 the Soho Society was formed, and the group launched a campaign to clean up the area; by the early 1980s all sex shops had to be licensed.

The area is now known primarily as the focus of London's LGBTQI+ scene and for its excellent clubs, restaurants and bars. The main locations to check out include Old Compton Street, the area's main artery, and Soho Square, an unexpected green space that gets very crowded in summer. There's also an authentic outdoor fruit-and-vegetable market in Berwick Street with bustling street-food stalls and, in the west, pedestrianised Carnaby Street, which although not at the cutting edge as it was in its 60s heyday is still worth a look for its colourful fashion boutiques.

At the southern edge of Soho is Shaftesbury Avenue, the heart of London's Theatreland. On the other side of the street is **Chinatown**, a tiny district that centres on Gerrard Street, with street names are subtitled in Chinese.

LEICESTER SQUARE

South of Chinatown is **Leicester Square** ❾, which can be accessed via Leicester Place, home to the arthouse Prince Charles cinema and the French church Notre Dame de France. The expansive square is dominated by big cinema complexes, where many of the capital's blockbuster premieres take place, alongside chain restaurants and mainstream nightclubs.

COVENT GARDEN

With its pedestrianised cobbled streets, markets, opera house, shops, theatres, cafés and bars, **Covent Garden** ❿ is one of central

London's most appealing areas. It has a lively atmosphere and attracts a mix of people including opera and theatregoers, street performers, shoppers and tourists.

The area owes its name to the fact that it was once pastureland belonging to the convent of Westminster Abbey. After the dissolution of the monasteries the land was given to the first Earl of Bedford, then in the late 1620s the Covent Garden that we see today took its form, when the fourth Earl commissioned Inigo Jones to design buildings 'fit for habitation'. Influenced by his studies of Palladian architecture in Italy, Jones created the main piazza, which consisted of St Paul's Church and three sides of terraced houses. Although the design found little favour with Jones's contemporaries, it attracted rich, aristocratic families.

However, Covent Garden's popularity as a chic residential area was short-lived. In 1670, Charles II granted a licence for flowers and vegetables to be sold here, and with the arrival of the market and the lower-class people it attracted, the area began a slow transformation. By the late eighteenth century it was best known for coffee shops, sex workers and brothels. The market was held here until 1974, when it moved to its present site in Vauxhall, south London.

The central **Market Hall** was designed by Charles Fowler in 1831. Today it hosts a selection of small shops, various arts and crafts market stalls, several bars and restaurants and various spaces where buskers perform. Street entertainers also utilise the space in front of **St Paul's Church** (www.actorschurch.org; free) on the western side of the square. St Paul's is known as the 'actors' church', owing to its long association with the many theatres in the parish, and it contains memorials to Charlie Chaplin, Noel Coward, Vivien Leigh and Gracie Fields.

At the northeast corner of Covent Garden is the **Royal Opera House** (www.rbo.org.uk), the third theatre to have stood on this site since 1732 (two previous buildings burnt down). The present

Street performer in Covent Garden

one, which dates from 1946, was refurbished for the millennium at a cost of £120 million; facilities for the performers were improved, air-conditioning was introduced into the auditorium, and the glass **Paul Hamlyn Hall** (a delightful place for coffee, originally known as the Floral Hall) was rebuilt next to the main house. Both opera and ballet are performed here.

Located in the southeast corner of the piazza, the **London Transport Museum** (www.ltmuseum.co.uk; ticket is valid for one year from purchase) utilises many interactive exhibits to trace the development of the city's buses, trams and tube since 1800, as well as exploring the future of public transport in the capital. They also offer excellent, award-winning **Hidden London** tours, which take you underground tube stations and through secret tunnels that were used during the wars.

Buckingham Palace

SOMERSET HOUSE

Just south of Covent Garden, parallel to the Thames, is the **Strand**, a road that links Westminster to the City along a route opened in Edward the Confessor's time. The church on an island at the eastern end of the Strand is **St Mary-le-Strand**. Built in 1724, it originally stood on the north side of the street, but, with the advent of the motorcar, the Strand was widened, and the church was left in odd isolation.

Opposite St Mary-le-Strand is **Somerset House** ⓫ (www.somersethouse.org.uk; free except special exhibitions), a grand example of neo-classicism, designed in the eighteenth century by Sir William Chambers. Located on the site of a sixteenth-century palace, Chambers' noble edifice was built to house government offices, including the Navy Board, and the three main learned societies of the United Kingdom: the Royal Academy of Arts, the Royal Society and the Society of Antiquaries. By the early twentieth century the building was mainly used as the headquarters of the Inland Revenue and the Registry of Births, Marriages and Deaths. In the 1970s it was decided to return it to public use – it is now home to an exhibition space dedicated to presenting contemporary arts in innovative ways. The central courtyard is a fabulous space, housing an ice-rink in winter and hosting live music performances and open-air cinema screenings in summer.

Also housed in the complex is the **Courtauld Institute of Art Gallery** (www.courtauld.ac.uk), a compact and impressive collection of Old Masters and Impressionist and Post-Impressionist works, including famous paintings by Manet, Cézanne, Degas, Monet, Renoir and Van Gogh.

THE EMBANKMENT

Parallel to the Strand is the riverside Embankment, which is the site of London's oldest outdoor monument, **Cleopatra's Needle**. Cut from the quarries of Aswan (c.1475 BC), the 68ft (21 metre) Egyptian obelisk is one of a pair (the other is in New York) and was given to the British Empire by the Turkish Viceroy of Egypt in 1819. It took 59 years for the British to move it from where it lay in the sand to its present position – it was intended to stand in front of the Houses of Parliament but the ground there was too unstable. It is said that the sphinxes at the base are facing in the wrong direction.

BUCKINGHAM PALACE AND MAYFAIR

HIGHLIGHTS

- » Buckingham Palace and the Parks, see page 50
- » St James's, see page 51
- » Mayfair, see page 53

West of Piccadilly Circus is the smartest part of central London. The area has consistently retained its social prestige since the building of its great estates began in the 1660s. With its Georgian residences, gentlemen's clubs and exclusive shops, it is synonymous with wealth. The area is divided in two by Piccadilly. To the north of this famous thoroughfare lies Mayfair, to the south St James's, the royal parks and Buckingham Palace.

BUCKINGHAM PALACE AND THE PARKS

Traditionally the monarch's main London residence, **Buckingham Palace** ⑫ (www.rct.uk) was originally built in 1702 for the Duke of Buckingham, then bought by George III and enlarged for George IV by the architect John Nash. The main facade is a later addition – by Aston Webb in 1913. King Charles III and Queen Camilla, who were crowned in 2023, reside mainly at nearby Clarence House and are due to relocate permanently to Buckingham Palace after a period of renovations. If the King is in residence at the palace, the royal standard flies from the central flagpole.

The building was opened to the public in 1993 to help pay for the repairs to the fire-ravaged Windsor Castle, and now partly opens in summer/early autumn when the King is away, with some exclusive guided tours (around £100 per person) held in winter. The nineteen State Rooms open to the public include the Dining Room, Music Room and Throne Room.

The King has one of the world's best private art collections, comprising about 9,000 works, including exceptional drawings by Leonardo da Vinci and royal portraits by Holbein and Van Dyck. A selection is on show in the **King's Gallery** (Buckingham Palace Road; www.rct.uk; closed Tues & Wed, last admission at 4.15pm).

Most people in the crowds outside Buckingham Palace come to see the **Changing the Guard**, at 11am most days. The New Guard, which marches up from Wellington Barracks, meets the Old Guard in the forecourt of the palace, and they exchange symbolic keys to the accompaniment of regimental music.

North of the palace is **Green Park** ⑬, the smallest of the royal parks and the only one without flower beds – hence the name. The park was once a burial ground for people affected by leprosy, and its lush grass is said to be a result of this.

Running east from Buckingham Palace is the Mall, the sweeping boulevard that edges **St James's Park** ⑭. The park is the oldest of the royal parks, built by Charles II, who had been exiled in France and wanted to recreate the formal gardens he had admired there. The bird sanctuary on Duck Island is now home to exotic waterfowl and pelicans (the legacy of a pair presented to Charles II by the Russian ambassador in 1665).

ST JAMES'S

St James's, the area north of the park, is the epitome of aristocratic London and the heart of the old-fashioned gentlemen's clubs. In its eighteenth-century heyday it was an upper-class male bastion; nowadays, there are very few gentlemen's clubs left, but the district is still home to centuries-old wine merchants, milliners, shirt-makers (notably on Jermyn Street) and shoemakers who cater for discerning masculine tastes.

St James's Palace (closed to the public), north of the Mall, was built as a hunting lodge in 1532 by Henry VIII. The palace was the official residence of the court before Buckingham Palace was first used for that purpose in 1837. It is now home to several members of the royal family, including the Princess Royal.

Also on the north side of the Mall, in Carlton Terrace, is the **Institute of Contemporary Arts**, or **ICA** (www.ica.art; free except special exhibitions). In addition to the gallery spaces, where changing art

St James's Palace, after which the area is named

BUCKINGHAM PALACE AND MAYFAIR

SHEPHERD MARKET

The pedestrianised enclave off Mayfair's Curzon Street (or via Clarges Street or Half Moon Street from Piccadilly) was named after Edward Shepherd, who built the area in the mid-eighteenth century. In the seventeenth century, the annual 15-day 'May Fair' was held here, hence the name of the whole area. Shepherd Market (www.shepherdmarket.com) is now a great place to relax, with bars, Victorian pubs and restaurants aplenty, many of which have pavement tables.

exhibitions are held, the centre is home to a decent café/restaurant, a bar (comedy and other events are sometimes staged here), a theatre, a tiny bookshop and two cinema screens, where arthouse movies are shown.

Beside the ICA, on the route to the east end of elegant Pall Mall, is the **Duke of York Column**, a memorial to George III's impecunious son, who was the Commander-in-Chief of the British Forces. The Duke died with debts of over £2 million, and the statue was paid for by withholding one day's pay from every officer and soldier. North of here is elegant **Pall Mall** where exclusive gentlemen's clubs mingle with the grand homes of royalty. Off the north side of Pall Mall is **St James's Square**, laid out by Henry Jermyn, the first Earl of St Alban in about 1660.

Parallel to Pall Mall, running west from Piccadilly Circus towards Hyde Park Corner, is **Piccadilly**. The road is one of the main routes in and out of the West End, and its name comes from the 'pickadills', or ruffs, worn by the dandies who frequented the area in the 1600s. At 197 Piccadilly is **St James's Church** (www.sjp.org.uk), designed in 1684 by Sir Christopher Wren. It has a craft market and coffee house and holds excellent classical concerts.

A few doors down is **Fortnum & Mason** ⓫ (www.fortnumandmason.com), London's most glamorous grocers and purveyor of goods to the Royal Family for over 300 years. Enjoy the quintessential

MAYFAIR

(if pricey) afternoon tea here or further along the road at **The Ritz** (www.theritzlondon.com; reservations essential; dress smartly).

MAYFAIR

To the north of Piccadilly is **Mayfair**, one of the classiest areas in the capital and the most expensive place to land on the English Monopoly board. The second most expensive, Park Lane, bounds the area to the west, while Oxford Street marks Mayfair's northern side. The district takes its name from a riotous seventeenth-century fair and still contains dozens of narrow alleys and cut-throughs that give the visitor a flavour of seventeenth-century London. It was at this time that the area was first transformed from a swampy plague pit where highwaymen preyed on passers-by to the fashionable place to be seen, and where Regency bucks such as Beau Brummell chaperoned respectable ladies on their morning strolls.

On Piccadilly is the seventeenth-century Burlington House, home of the **Royal Academy of Arts** ⓰, or RA, (www.royalacademy.org.uk), entered through a huge arch and across a large courtyard and known for high-profile temporary exhibitions. Its less-known permanent collection includes Constable's *The Leaping Horse*, Gainsborough's *A Romantic Landscape with Sheep at a Spring*, Laura Knight's *A Misty*

Mayfair's Burlington Arcade

Sunrise and Tracey Emin's *Trying to Find You 1*. Diploma work, submitted by Academicians on election to membership, includes Walter Sickert's *Santa Maria delle Salute*, Richard Eurich's *The Mariner's Return*, David Hockney's *A Closer Grand Canyon* and Sonia Boyce's *We Move in Her Way: Dancers*. Built as part of a renovation project to mark its 250th anniversary, Weston Bridge links Burlington House to additional gallery space and a lecture theatre in Burlington Gardens.

Alongside the RA is the **Burlington Arcade**, built in 1815 and one of the oldest, most elegant of the capital's covered shopping promenades. Beadles patrol this Regency promenade. In their top hats and livery, they ensure good behaviour, with 'no undue whistling, humming or hurrying'.

Mayfair's other upmarket retail environments include the bespoke suits of **Savile Row**, the commercial art galleries of **Cork Street**, auction houses Sotheby's and Bonhams, and **Old Bond Street** and **New Bond Street**, both of which are famous for their proliferation of designer flagship stores. Off New Bond Street is Brook Street – at No. 25 is **Handel Hendrix House** (www.handelhendrix.org; charge), where the composer of *The Messiah* lived from 1723 until his death in 1759. Next door, much later (1968–9) lived a very different musician – Jimi Hendrix – whose upper floor flat opened to the public in 2016; a general ticket allows access to both residences. Off Brook Street – at No. 8 Davies Street – is Bastian, the first London outpost of the esteemed contemporary art gallery in Berlin.

BLOOMSBURY AND MARYLEBONE

HIGHLIGHTS

- » The British Museum, see page 55
- » King's Cross and St Pancras, see page 56
- » The Regent's Park, see page 58
- » Marylebone, see page 59

Despite their central location, both Marylebone and Bloomsbury are surprisingly genteel. Marylebone High Street and Marylebone Lane enjoy a village atmosphere, and many of London's top doctors have surgeries around Harley Street and Wimpole Street. East of Tottenham Court Road is Bloomsbury, London's literary heart and home to the British Museum, British Library and much of the University of London.

British Museum

THE BRITISH MUSEUM

The **British Museum** ⑰ (Great Russell Street; www.britishmuseum. org; free), opened in 1759, is the nation's largest museum with at least 8 million items from around the world, from Neolithic antiquities to twentieth-century manuscripts. The main entrance is via the steel-and-glass-roofed Great Court, Europe's largest covered space, in the middle of which is the grand former main reading room, now an information centre. Behind the famous Athenian frontage are the controversial fifth-century BC Elgin Marbles, 'rescued' by Lord Elgin from the Parthenon in Athens in 1801, and the linguist's codebook, the Rosetta Stone, the key that unlocked the mysteries of ancient Egyptian hieroglyphics. There are excellent Assyrian, Egyptian and Roman artefacts in the main museum, including the world's richest collection of Egyptian mummies and funerary art, the exquisite first-century Roman Portland Vase and the

LITERARY BLOOMSBURY

In the early twentieth century Bloomsbury was home to Virginia Woolf, Vanessa Bell, Duncan Grant, Dora Carrington, Roger Fry and Queen Victoria's biographer, Lytton Strachey, known collectively as the 'Bloomsbury set'. Although their inclinations spread across painting, philosophy and writing, their connection was to challenge the conventions of the day. At that time publishing was a major industry in the area, with publishers including the Bloomsbury set's own Hogarth Press. Many imprints have since moved to cheaper premises, however, as have most of the area's second-hand bookstores.

Nereid Monument, an elaborate Turkish tomb dating from 380 BC. Also worth seeing are the Prints and Drawings rooms, which hold graphic works by artists ranging from Albrecht Dürer and Francisco Goya to Paula Rego, Grayson Perry and Kara Walker.

Though a world museum, it is guardian of the great British treasures, too, including the Sutton Hoo trove from a burial ship of an Anglo-Saxon king, the seventh-century Lindisfarne Gospels and Lindow Man, a Briton killed two thousand years ago and preserved in a peat bog.

Continuing north towards King's Cross divert east to 48 Doughty Street and the **Charles Dickens Museum** (www.dickensmuseum.com; charge). The author lived here from 1837–9 while writing *Nicholas Nickleby* and *Oliver Twist*. It is the only one of his London homes still standing, and exhibits all manner of memorabilia: his letters, manuscripts, desk, locks of his hair and even his lemon squeezer.

KING'S CROSS AND ST PANCRAS

The area around King's Cross and St Pancras stations has been completely regenerated in recent years, with the fully overhauled **St Pancras International** itself one of the architectural and retail highlights of the area. The immense Victorian Gothic red-brick and

KING'S CROSS AND ST PANCRAS

glass edifice is London's Eurostar terminus, while the adjacent St Pancras hotel has been restored to its former glory. Next door, King's Cross has also been improved, with a semi-circular concourse in the station itself. Nearby, it is worth visiting the vast, canal-side Granary Square, where one thousand choreographed, illuminated fountains shoot up daily between 8am and 7pm. The UK's first and only LGBTQI+ museum, **Queer Britain** (2 Granary Square; www.queerbritain.org.uk; free), opened in 2022, sits on the square and has exhibitions, events and an incredible archive dedicated to LGBTQI+ history and culture. Just behind the square is the Coal Drops Yard development, a high-end shopping and dining space in converted warehouses under a striking curved roof structure, and the **Lightroom** gallery (www.lightroom.co.uk; charge), opened in 2023, a huge four-storey space showcasing state-of-the-art, visually immersive exhibitions, from the works of David Hockney to space exploration with Tom Hanks to the history of *Vogue* and the runway.

The **British Library** (96 Euston Road; www.bl.uk; free) used to be housed in the British Museum, but as the museum collection grew, it was decided to move the 9 million books, including a Gutenberg Bible, the Magna Carta and original texts by Shakespeare and Dickens. Galleries in

One of the taller inhabitants of London Zoo

the current premises, near St Pancras, display some of the library's treasures, ranging from a third-century biblical manuscript to original copies of Beatles' lyrics. The library hosts changing literary-themed exhibitions, many of which are free, and has five places to eat and drink.

West of here on Euston Road is the **Wellcome Collection** (www.wellcomecollection.org; free), a health and medicine museum which showcases an eclectic mix of art, books and medical artefacts, including a replica shrunken head, a chastity belt and Napoleon Bonaparte's toothbrush.

THE REGENT'S PARK

Further west still is **The Regent's Park** ⓲, an elegant 470-acre (190-hectare) space surrounded by smart Regency terraces. Within the park are formal gardens, an open-air theatre where plays, including Shakespeare, are staged in summer, and a boating lake. Regent's Canal runs through the north of the park – if you have a few hours, you can take a scenic walk all the way along the length of the canal from east to west, hitting many of London's central sights en route. Also at the northern end of the park is **London Zoo** (www.zsl.org/zsl-london-zoo; charge), which is home to more than 660 species of animal. There are lions, tigers, gorillas and hippos, with many breeding programmes for endangered species, including Tiger Territory and the Land of the Lions, which is home to five endangered Asiatic lions. The zoo is expensive, but discount offers, including 2-for-1 entrance with a train ticket, can help bring down the price.

Northwest of Regent's Park is **Lord's Cricket Ground** (www.lords.org), the ancestral home of cricket. To visit the ground, the portrait-lined Long Room through which players walk on their way to the field, and the memorabilia-packed MCC Museum, you have to take a 100-minute tour (charge), which runs most days except on important match days.

MARYLEBONE

South of the Regent's Park is **Madame Tussauds** (www.madametussauds.co.uk/london; charge). The waxworks museum is home to thousands of effigies of various celebrities from royals to film stars to Marvel superheroes, made with glass-fibre bodies and wax heads. It was founded in 1835 by Marie Tussaud, who prepared death masks of famous victims of the guillotine during the French Revolution. Those gory beginnings are echoed in the Chamber of Horrors.

Nearby at 221b Baker Street is the **Sherlock Holmes Museum** (www.sherlock-holmes.co.uk; charge). It pays tribute to Sir Arthur Conan Doyle's fictitious sleuth by creating an imaginative evocation of the Victorian detective's apartment.

Other cultural attractions in Marylebone include the Art Nouveau **Wigmore Hall** (36 Wigmore Street; www.wigmore-hall.org.uk), a notable venue for chamber music, and the **Wallace Collection** ⓲ (Hertford House, Manchester Square; www.wallacecollection.org; free except for some special exhibitions), a fine private collection of seventeenth- and eighteenth-century English and European paintings, porcelain and furniture, elegantly displayed in an eighteenth-century mansion. Highlights include Franz Hals' The Laughing Cavalier, Jean-Honoré Fragonard's The Swing and furniture attributed to master cabinetmaker André-Charles Boulle.

The London Eye, seen from Westminster Bridge

THE SOUTH BANK

HIGHLIGHTS

- » County Hall, see page 61
- » The London Eye, see page 62
- » The Southbank Centre, see page 62
- » Around Waterloo, see page 63
- » Around Gabriel's Wharf, see page 64
- » Tate Modern, see page 64
- » The Millennium Bridge, see page 65
- » Shakespeare's Globe, see page 66
- » Southwark, see page 67
- » Tower Bridge, see page 64
- » Butlers Wharf, see page 71

The area south of the Thames, from County Hall (opposite Westminster) to Southwark, further east, is an historic part of London. The first bridge across the Thames was built by the Romans near London Bridge, and the community around it developed as an alternative to the City, since it lay beyond the City's jurisdiction. In Shakespeare's day this was a place for showing unlicensed plays and setting up brothels, and it retained its reputation as an area of vice well into the nineteenth century.

In the late twentieth century the area was transformed into a vibrant cultural centre; warehouses were renovated and converted into expensive flats, and the Underground's Jubilee Line extension improved access. Highlights of the area now include the London Eye, South Bank Centre, National Theatre, BFI film complex, Tate Modern and Shakespeare's Globe. Further east, the capital's (and Western Europe's) tallest building, The Shard, has led regeneration of the London Bridge area. Located beside London Bridge station, at 1,016ft (310m) tall, it contains several restaurants, the 5-star *Shangri-La* hotel, offices and a viewing gallery (see page 68).

COUNTY HALL

Facing the Houses of Parliament is the neoclassical **County Hall**, built from 1909–22 and once the seat of the Greater London Council, which ran London until an unsympathetic Thatcher government abolished it in 1986. It now houses two hotels, several restaurants and various family attractions. The **Sea Life London Aquarium** (www.visitsealife.com/london; charge) contains thousands of specimens representing around 500 species of fish in 15 themed zones. The **London Dungeon** (www.thedungeons.com/london/en; charge) is a theme park of gore, focussing on London's bloody history. Shrek's Adventure (www.shreksadventure.com; charge) is a walk- and ride-through experience that allows you to mingle with characters from the famous movie.

Imperial War Museum

THE LONDON EYE

Towering over County Hall is the **London Eye** [20] (www.londoneye.com; charge). Europe's tallest observation wheel was built to mark the turn of the millennium. At 450ft (135m), it is one of the highest structures in London. The 32 enclosed capsules, each holding 25 people, take 30 minutes to make a full rotation – a speed slow enough to allow passengers to step in and out while the wheel keeps moving. On a clear day, you can see for 25 miles (40km).

THE SOUTHBANK CENTRE

East along the river from the London Eye is the **Southbank Centre** [21], an iconic brutalist building and Europe's largest arts complex, housing concert halls, a gallery, cinema and theatre (www.southbankcentre.co.uk). Developments in the 2000s greatly improved the area around the centre, which is now packed with lively restaurants and bars. The **Royal Festival Hall**, the only permanent building designed for the 1951 Festival of Britain, is a major music venue, host to many music, literary and cultural events throughout the year, and the home of the National Poetry Library.

In 1967 the 2,900-seat hall gained two neighbours: the 917-seater Queen Elizabeth Hall, for chamber concerts, music theatre and opera, and the more intimate, 372-seat Purcell Room. On the upper level of the Southbank Centre complex is the **Hayward Gallery**. The gallery's programme of changing exhibitions focuses on single artists, historical themes and artistic movements, other cultures, and contemporary themes.

Next door is **BFI Southbank** (www.bfi.org.uk), Britain's leading art-house cinema since 1952. With four screens, the biggest film library in the world, an interactive 'mediathèque' and a riverfront bar and café, it holds over 2,400 annual screenings and events, from silent movies (some with live piano accompaniment) to world cinema, and the annual London Film Festival in October.

The final building in the complex is the **National Theatre** (www.nationaltheatre.org.uk). Opened in 1976, it houses three separate theatres under one roof: the 1,150-seater Olivier, the 890-seater Lyttelton and the intimate Dorfman with 450 seats and galleries on three sides.

AROUND WATERLOO

A detour away from the South Bank along Waterloo Road takes you past the cylindrical **BFI IMAX Cinema** (www.bfi.org.uk/bfi-imax), the largest cinema screen in the UK. Where Waterloo Road meets The Cut is the **Old Vic** theatre (www.oldvictheatre.com), founded in 1818. A music hall in its early days, it is now a repertory theatre. Further along The Cut, the **Young Vic** (www.youngvic.org) stages experimental plays and gives young directors a chance to develop their art.

Inside the Tate Modern

South of Waterloo station is the **Imperial War Museum** ㉒ (Lambeth Road; www.iwm.org.uk; free), which underwent a £40m refurbishment in 2014 to coincide with the 100th anniversary of the start of World War I. There are several galleries dedicated to the World Wars, the Holocaust, and to art, film and photography, and the building's famous atrium houses war relics including a Spitfire and a Harrier Jump Jet.

Located in the 1811 Bethlehem hospital for the insane, there is much civilian material from both world wars on display at the museum, plus the latest in weaponry. An audio-visual display recreates a wartime air raid on a London street, and visitors can experience conditions in the trenches during World War I. The museum's Holocaust Exhibition is built around the testimonies of survivors, from the origins of anti-Semitism to its horrific conclusion.

AROUND GABRIEL'S WHARF

East of the National Theatre is **Gabriel's Wharf**, a group of shops and restaurants backed by a striking set of *trompe l'œil* paintings. Set back from the river, the Art Deco **OXO Tower** has pinprick windows outlining the word 'Oxo', a gimmick that the makers of the beef extract of the same name designed to get round a ban on riverfront advertising. The tower has a public viewing gallery and an excellent restaurant.

Further east, just beyond Blackfriars Bridge, which is home to Blackfriars station, the riverside walk leads past the **Bankside Gallery** (www.banksidegallery.com; free), home of the Royal Watercolour Society and Royal Society of Painter-Printmakers.

TATE MODERN

Easily identifiable by its tall brick chimney, **Tate Modern** ㉓ (Bankside; www.tate.org.uk; free except for special exhibitions) occupies the former Bankside Power Station and houses the Tate's international modern collection and part of its contemporary collection. The main entrance, to the west of the building, leads into the ground floor through a broad sweep of glass doors and then down a massive concrete ramp. The impressive space rising six storeys ahead is the Turbine Hall, the old boiler room now used to house massive art installations. A bridge across the Turbine Hall links level four with the Blavatnik Building, designed, like the gallery's first phase, by renowned architects Herzog & de Meuron. Its

THE MILLENNIUM BRIDGE

twisted pyramid shape, with a facade of latticed brickwork and folded surfaces, adds a new dimension to London's skyline and there are stunning views from the roof terrace and restaurant.

The permanent collection, including work by Picasso, Matisse, Duchamp, Dalí, Bacon, Rego, Emin and Warhol, plus sculpture by Giacometti, Hepworth and Epstein, is displayed in four suites over two floors. On level 2 you will find 'Artist and Society' where the focus is how artists relate to the society in which they live; look out for works by Farah Al Qasimi and Piet Mondrian. Also on level 2 are the 'In the Studio' rooms with displays on artists' studio practices. One level 3 you'll find art and photography in the 'Performer and Participant' exhibition, while on level 4 are 'Materials and Objects' showcasing artists exploring forms and textures, and 'Media Networks' which looks at the way artists have responded to the constant changes in technology. To beat the crowds, visit on Friday or Saturday evening.

THE MILLENNIUM BRIDGE

Providing a link across the Thames from Tate Modern to St Paul's, as well as some spectacular views up and down the river, is Norman Foster's **Millennium Bridge**. Said to resemble a 'blade of light' when floodlit, this innovative suspension bridge – its cables are strung horizontally rather than vertically – opened in 2000.

The Thames Path

SHAKESPEARE'S GLOBE

Bankside and Southwark are the South Bank's most historic areas. They grew up in competition with the City across the river, but by the sixteenth century had become dens of vice. Bankside was famous for brothels, bear- and bull-baiting pits, prize fights and the first playhouses, including **Shakespeare's Globe** (21 New Globe Walk; www.shakespearesglobe.com; tours available, charge). The replica of the 1599 building opened in 1996 and is worth a visit even if you're not seeing a play. Thanks to the efforts of the actor Sam Wanamaker, who sadly died before the project was completed, the Globe has been re-created using original construction methods. The open-air galleried theatre accommodates 1,500 people – 600 standing (and liable to get wet if

Fresh produce at Borough Market

it rains) and 900 seated. The season runs mid-Apr–mid-Oct but plays can also be seen year-round at the exquisite indoor Sam Wanamaker Playhouse.

Shakespeare's plays were not only shown at the Globe but also at the **Rose Theatre** (www.rosetheatre.org.uk), Bankside's first playhouse, built in 1587, but pulled down in the early seventeenth century. The foundations were discovered in 1989 and a campaign to restore it began. The Rose reopened in 1999 and today the indoor archaeological site can be visited during special events, check the events calendar on the website for details.

SOUTHWARK

Back on the riverside walk, by Southwark Bridge, is the **Anchor Inn**. The present building (1770–5), rebuilt after the Great Fire of London, is the sole survivor of the 22 busy inns that once lined Bankside. Just behind a single gable wall are the remains of **Winchester Palace**, the former thirteenth-century London residence of the Bishop of Winchester. There's not much left to see, but the brick ruins and large rose window are quite pretty and atmospheric, with flowerbeds nestled among the foundations. The powerful bishops had their own laws, regulated local brothels and were the first authority in England to lock up miscreants. The prison they founded, in Clink Street, remained a lock-up until the eighteenth century, and the word 'clink' became a euphemism for jail. The **Clink Prison Museum** (1 Clink Street; www.clink.co.uk; charge) recalls the area's seedy past.

Clink Street leads to Pickfords Wharf, built in 1864 for storing hops, flour and seeds. At the end of the street, in the St Mary Overie Dock, is a full-size replica of Sir Francis Drake's sixteenth-century galleon, the **Golden Hinde** (Clink Street; www.goldenhinde.com; charge to go onboard). The ship, launched in 1973, is the only replica to have completed a circumnavigation of the globe. It has now clocked up more nautical miles than the original.

Southwark Cathedral and Borough

Southwest of London Bridge and hemmed in by the railway, is **Southwark Cathedral** ㉔ (http://cathedral.southwark.anglican.org; free). In the twelfth century it was a priory church, and it has a Norman north door, early Gothic work and a number of medieval ornaments. Shakespeare was a parishioner here, and a memorial in the south aisle, paid for by public subscription in 1912, shows him reclining in front of a frieze of sixteenth-century Bankside; above it is a modern stained-glass window depicting characters from his plays. John Harvard, who gave his name to the American university, was baptised here, and is commemorated in the Harvard Chapel.

Near the cathedral is **Borough Market** (www.boroughmarket.org.uk), which despite its smart glass and steel frontage on Borough High Street, dates back to the thirteenth century. Now a lively gourmet market (and an incredibly popular tourist destination), it has over 100 stalls, many offering high-quality takeaway meals and fresh produce, intermingled with a host of bars and restaurants. The market is open six days a week (closed Mon), and it isn't cheap, but the quality is high and you can often try before you buy. Apart from organic basics such as fruit and vegetables, and fresh fish, there is a wide choice of international food, with stalls specialising in cured meats and European cheeses, Middle Eastern mezze, Indian street food, Spanish tapas and more. It's also fun to explore the adjacent, newer **Borough Yards** development under the railway arches, home to more eateries and some stylish shops.

Across Borough High Street from the cathedral, the **Old Operating Theatre and Herb Garret** (9a St Thomas Street; www.oldoperatingtheatre.com; charge) is Britain's only surviving nineteenth-century operating theatre, now a museum. The Herb Garret, once a store and curing place for herbs, now documents their use in nineteenth-century medicine.

East along St Thomas Street is the Western Europe's tallest building, **The Shard** ㉕. Designed by Renzo Piano, the behemoth towers

Viewing platform at The Shard

1,016ft (310 metres) over London Bridge station next door and has sparked massive regeneration in the area. If you have a head for heights, you can take a lift up to the 72nd floor (entrance on Joiner Street; www.theviewfromtheshard.com; charge) for unobstructed views of the city and beyond. Advance booking is recommended, although it is sensible to check the weather first, as mist (particularly in the mornings) often clouds the upper part of the tower.

For excellent food and drink options, continue east for a couple of minutes, to reach Bermondsey Street. This fashionable strip is also home to Zandra Rhodes' colourful **Fashion and Textile Museum** (83 Bermondsey Street; http://fashiontextilemuseum.org; charge) which puts on changing exhibitions exploring fashion, textiles and jewellery – past exhibitions have covered fashion renegades from 1980s London, and textiles by Andy Warhol. Further

The Royal Courts of Justice

along the street, at No. 144–152, is **White Cube** (http://whitecube.com; free), the largest of the celebrity gallery owner Jay Jopling's sites and an iconic minimalist space, which has featured contemporary art exhibitions by the likes of Tracey Emin, Gilbert & George, and Christian Marclay.

The Pool of London
Between London Bridge and Tower Bridge is the Upper Pool of London, a former hive of waterborne trade. **Hay's Galleria**, with its shops, stalls and restaurants, marks the first of the Surrey Docks on the south bank. **HMS Belfast**, a World War II cruiser, is moored here as a museum (www.iwm.org.uk/visits/hms-belfast; charge). To its east, the oval-shaped glass building is **City Hall**, home to the Mayor of London and the Greater London Authority (the body that governs London).

TOWER BRIDGE

The elaborate Gothic-style bridge looming into sight as you walk east is **Tower Bridge** ㉖. In the nineteenth century, a time of great industrial expansion, there was a need to improve circulation over the river without hindering the access of ships into London's docks. The result was this triumph of Victorian engineering, built between 1886 and 1894, a bridge that could be raised, made from a steel frame held together with 3 million rivets and clad with decorative stonework. The bridge was opened amid great celebration by the then-Prince and Princess of Wales, on June 30, 1894. The entrance to the **Tower Bridge Exhibition** (www.towerbridge.org.uk; charge) is on the north bank of the Thames. The semi-guided tour takes visitors through the bridge's history, from the controversy that raged over the need to construct it, to its electrification in 1977. You also get the chance to see much of the inside of the bridge, including the engine rooms and raised, glass-floor walkways.

BUTLERS WHARF

The old warehouses located just east of Tower Bridge contain a gourmet's delight. The gourmet in question is Habitat founder Sir Terence Conran, who has opened up several restaurants in the biscuit-coloured **Butlers Wharf**. Originally completed in 1873, and once the largest warehouse complex on the Thames, Butlers Wharf closed in 1972. In 1985 a development team chaired by Conran began transforming the area's buildings into a stylish shopping, dining and residential area at a cost of £100 million.

THE CITY

HIGHLIGHTS

- » Legal London, see page 72
- » St Paul's Cathedral, see page 73
- » The Barbican, see page 74
- » The Financial City, see page 75
- » The Tower of London, see page 77

For most of the capital's 2,000-year history, the area between St Paul's and the Tower – generally referred to as the 'Square Mile' – was London. Still known as 'The City', it has its own local government, led by a Lord Mayor, and its own police force. The network of medieval alleys and back streets is still evident, but today's tall buildings hum with banks of computers processing international finance. Teeming with life on weekdays, the City is virtually deserted at weekends.

The Square Mile extends from the highly ornate Law Courts (located at the junction of the Strand and Fleet Street) to the west, to the Tower of London to the east, and from the Barbican in the north to the Thames to the south. This was the area originally enclosed by the Roman Wall, but it is now firmly held in place by commerce.

LEGAL LONDON

Legal London starts at the edge of the City with the **Royal Courts of Justice** (better known as the Law Courts), in an elaborate late nineteenth-century building on the Strand. On the other side of busy Fleet Street, a few steps along, a tiny alleyway leads to the gas-lit sanctuary of the area known as the Temple, which houses two of the four Inns of Court – Inner Temple and Middle Temple (not open to the public). In former times these were the residences of barristers and barristers-in-training, and today's barristers-in-training must still be members of an Inn. The Temple takes its name from its twelfth- and thirteenth-century function as the home of the crusading Knights Templar.

On Chancery Lane is Lincoln's Inn, the oldest of the four Inns of Court. On a large square adjacent is **Sir John Soane's Museum** (13 Lincoln's Inn Fields; www.soane.org; Soane Lates last Fri of month; free except Lates), the former home of a prominent late eighteenth-century London architect. The house is just as Soane left it, packed from floor to ceiling with priceless treasures, such as paintings by Hogarth (notably *The Rake's Progress* series), Turner and Canaletto.

Off Fleet Street, famous as the former centre of English newspaper production, is **Dr Samuel Johnson's House** (17 Gough Square; www.drjohnsonshouse.org; charge). It was here that Samuel Johnson lived from 1748 to 1759, compiling his dictionary in the garret with six poor copyists.

ST PAUL'S CATHEDRAL

St Paul's ❷ (www.stpauls.co.uk; free to attend services, charge for tours), the first purpose-built Protestant cathedral, is Sir Christopher Wren's greatest work. A tablet above Wren's plain marble tomb in the crypt reads: *Lector, si monumentum requiris, circumspice* (Reader, if you wish to see his memorial, look around you). Although Westminster Abbey hosts more national occasions, Churchill lay in state here in 1965, and Prince Charles married Diana Spencer here in 1981.

Spectacular St Paul's Cathedral

Historians believe that the first church on this site was built in the seventh century, although it came into its own as Old St Paul's only in the fourteenth century. By the sixteenth century St Paul's was the tallest cathedral in England. Much of the building was destroyed in the Great Fire of 1666. Construction on the new St Paul's Cathedral began in 1675, when Wren was 43.

The architect was an old man of 78 when his son Christopher finally laid the highest stone of the lantern on the central cupola in 1710. In total, the cathedral cost £747,954 to build, and most of the money was raised through taxing coal arriving at the port of London. The building is massive and the Portland stone dome alone – exceeded in size only by St Peter's in Rome – weighs over 50,000 tons. Generations have giggled secret messages in St Paul's

The Barbican Estate

Whispering Gallery, over 100ft (30m) of perfect acoustics. You have to climb 257 steps to reach it, however, and a further 270 to enjoy the view from the highest of the dome's three galleries.

In the cathedral's crypt, the largest vault of its kind in Europe, is a treasury containing ceremonial vessels, a burial chamber and a chapel dedicated to members of the Order of the British Empire (OBE). The highlights of this cavernous undercroft include the tombs of the Duke of Wellington (whose casket was so huge that it had to be lowered into its resting place via a hole in the Cathedral floor) and of Admiral Lord Nelson, who was foresighted enough to take a coffin with him to the Battle of Trafalgar.

THE BARBICAN

North of the City is the concrete **Barbican** ❷❽ (Silk Street; www.barbican.org.uk; free except for some special events), an arts and conference centre opened in 1982. The cultural offerings here include art galleries, theatres, a concert hall (the Barbican is the home of the London Symphony Orchestra), cinema, a library, bars and restaurants. You can also visit the Barbican's huge conservatory (the second largest in London), a vibrant, tranquil space with over 1,500 species of plants and trees.

Just outside the arts centre is the **Museum of London** (150

London Wall; www.museumoflondon.org.uk; free), which charts every aspect of the capital's long history.

THE FINANCIAL CITY

The heart of the business district of the City focuses on the **Bank of England** ㉙ (nicknamed 'The Old Lady of Threadneedle Street'). Imposing windowless walls rise impregnably, with seven stories above ground and three below. This is where the nation's gold reserves are kept. Opposite the Bank of England is the neoclassical **Mansion House**, residence of the Lord Mayor of London. Adjacent is Wren's **St Stephen Walbrook**, whose dome is said to have been a rehearsal for St Paul's.

Northwest of the Bank is the **Guildhall** (Basinghall Street; www.guildhall.cityoflondon.gov.uk; opening times vary subject to events taking place; free), the town hall of the City of London. This building dates from 1411 and withstood the Great Fire and the Blitz. Step inside when open to the public to see the ancient Great Hall. Here the centuries-old functions and ceremonies continue: banquets of state, the annual swearing-in of the

— **NOTES** —

A magnificent view of London's skyline can be seen from the building at 20 Fenchurch Street, known as the 'Walkie Talkie' due to its distinctive shape. The **Sky Garden** (https://skygarden.london) at the top, London's highest public garden, offers a sweeping panoramic of the city, with excellent photo opportunities and views of other buildings with famous nicknames such as the Leadenhall Building, known as the 'Cheesegrater'. Although 30 St Mary Axe is another of the City's most iconic sights, that name alone means little to most; more familiar is its nickname, 'The Gherkin', inspired by the tower's elongated shape and glass panels. The Sky Garden is free to visit but it's best to book your ticket in advance, especially if you want sunset views.

Leadenhall Market

new Lord Mayor in November and meetings of the Court of Common Council. The adjacent Art Gallery (free) is well worth a visit too – the remains of a Roman amphitheatre are visible on the lower floor.

East of the Bank of England, along the ancient thoroughfares of Cornhill and Leadenhall Street, is **Lloyd's of London**. Lloyd's originated in 1688 in Edward Lloyd's Coffee House, where ships' captains, owners and merchants gathered to do marine insurance deals. Lloyd's moved to Richard Rogers' space-age building in 1986. A huge atrium rises 200ft (60m) at the heart of this steel-and-glass structure which, like Rogers' Pompidou Centre, exposes its workings to view.

In the shadow of Lloyd's is the Victorian **Leadenhall Market** (https://leadenhallmarket.co.uk), once the wholesale market for poultry and game, and now a handsome commercial centre. It has been prettified, and its magnificent Victorian cream-and-maroon structure now houses sandwich bars, restaurants and upmarket fashion chain stores, which attract city workers at breakfast and lunchtime.

South of Leadenhall Market, back towards the river, is Christopher Wren's 202ft (62 metre) high **Monument** (Monument Yard; www.themonument.org.uk; charge to climb to the viewing platform), topped with a gleaming gold urn of fire. The Roman Doric column was designed to commemorate the victims of the Great Fire, which destroyed 13,200 houses and 87 churches. Its height matches the distance from the spot in Pudding Lane, where the fire is believed to have started. There are 311 stairs up to the encaged viewing platform at the top.

THE TOWER OF LONDON

East of the Monument, on the north bank of the Thames is the **Tower of London** ❸⓿ (Tower Hill; www.hrp.org.uk; charge). Encircled by a moat (now dry) and with 22 towers, the building was begun by William the Conqueror in 1078. Over the years its buildings have served as a fort, arsenal, palace and prison, and housed a treasury, public record office, observatory, royal mint and zoo.

At the centre of the complex is the White Tower, designed by the Norman monk Gandulf for William the Conqueror. The Tower's walls are 15ft (5m) thick and contain the fine Norman Chapel of St John on the first floor. Henry VIII added the domestic architecture of the Queen's House behind the Tower on the left, which is where the Tower's governor lives. The nineteenth-century Museum and Waterloo Barracks, to the right of the Tower, contain the Jewel House where the **Crown Jewels** are a major attraction. At the centre of the display are a dozen crowns and a glittering array of swords, sceptres and orbs. The Imperial State Crown, made in 1937, has 2,868 diamonds and is topped with an eleventh-century sapphire. A moving walkway speeds you past the treasures, so, rather disappointingly, you can't linger.

Look out for the Tower ravens (there are currently seven of them); according to legend, if they ever leave, the Tower and England will fall. Ravens are bred and their wings are clipped to ensure they stay. Also look out for the Beefeaters, who guard the tower and act as guides.

KENSINGTON AND CHELSEA

HIGHLIGHTS
- » Hyde Park and Kensington Gardens, see page 78
- » Kensington, see page 81
- » South Kensington, see page 83
- » Knightsbridge, see page 85
- » Chelsea, see page 86

The Royal Borough of Kensington and Chelsea is central London's most expensive residential area. It is home to upmarket shops such as Harrods and Harvey Nichols, designer row Sloane Street, and also takes in the King's Road, an influential fashion stretch in the 1960s. The borough has a royal palace, a fine park and a clutch of world-renowned museums.

HYDE PARK AND KENSINGTON GARDENS

Hyde Park and the adjoining Kensington Gardens cover one square mile (2.5 sq km) – the same area as the City of London. Although they are a single open space, they are two distinct parks, divided by the Ring or West Carriage Drive.

Hyde Park Corner, at the western end of Piccadilly, is a good place to enter the park. Near the entrance to the park, facing **Wellington Arch**, is Apsley House; although its official address is 149 Piccadilly, it also lays claim to the enviable address of No. 1, London, as it was the first house you'd reach on the main road into London back in the 1700s. Built by Robert Adam for the Duke of Wellington, it is now home to the **Wellington Collection** (www.wellington collection.co.uk; charge) and has a fine collection of Old Master paintings and memorabilia linked with the Duke. Highlights include Canova's larger-than-life nude statue of Napoleon, one of numerous items in his house depicting the Duke's great foe, and a magnificent reconstruction of the Waterloo Banquet.

The Domesday Book of 1086 records that wild bulls and boars once inhabited **Hyde Park** ㉛. The park was first owned by the monks of Westminster Abbey, but after ecclesiastic property was confiscated during the Dissolution of the Monasteries, Henry VIII turned it into a royal hunting ground. The park was opened to the public in the seventeenth century and then sold off in chunks by Oliver Cromwell, the Lord Protector.

Boating on the Serpentine, Hyde Park

At the northeast corner of the park is the monumental **Marble Arch**, erected in 1827 in front of Buckingham Palace and moved here in 1851 when it proved too narrow for the State coaches to pass through. The traffic island in which it now resides was the site of Tyburn Tree, a triangular gallows on which an estimated 50,000 people were publicly hanged between 1571 and 1759. Just inside the park is **Speakers' Corner**, where anyone can pull up a soap box and sound off – a tradition going back to the days when condemned men were allowed to have a last word.

KENSINGTON AND CHELSEA

In 2024, the internationally renowned **Moco Museum**, with branches already in Amsterdam and Barcelona, opened just in front of the Marble Arch (1 Marble Arch; www.london.mocomuseum.com; charge), which showcases some cutting-edge, immersive exhibitions of works by artists such as Kusama, Banksy and Basquiat. Just around the corner is **FRAMELESS** (6 Marble Arch; www.frameless.com; charge), which opened in 2022 and allows you to walk through galleries enjoying a stunning immersive experience of some of the world's most iconic art, from Van Gogh to Kandinsky.

The lake at the centre of both Hyde Park and Kensington Gardens is called the **Serpentine** in Hyde Park and the **Long Water** in Kensington Gardens. It was created in the 1730s as a boating pond, and boats can still be hired from the north bank. On the Kensington Gardens side, next to the lake, is a statue of J.M. Barrie's **Peter Pan**. It was made by George Frampton in 1912 and commissioned by Barrie himself, who used to live over the road. According to tradition, at 9am every Christmas Day, hardy swimmers dive into the lake to compete for the Peter Pan Cup. On the south side of the Serpentine is the **Diana, Princess of Wales Memorial Fountain**, a circular ring of flowing water that you can dip your feet in. Just west and north of the fountain are the **Serpentine Galleries**

The Royal Albert Hall

(www.serpentinegalleries.org; free). Serpentine South, housed in a 1930s teahouse, stages cutting-edge art shows, with past subjects including Man Ray, Henry Moore and Cindy Sherman. A short walk away is the Serpentine North gallery, a futuristic-looking building designed by architect Zaha Hadid and incorporating *The Magazine*, a listed neoclassical gunpowder store dating from 1805, now a restaurant (temporarily closed at the time of writing).

South of the gallery is the **Albert Memorial**, a gilded tribute to Queen Victoria's consort. Designed by Sir George Gilbert Scott, it depicts the Prince as a god or philosopher, holding the catalogue of the Great Exhibition. Opposite, just outside the park, is another of Victoria's tokens to her husband, the **Royal Albert Hall** (Kensington Gore; www.royalalberthall.com; charge for tours). There are various themed tours of the ornate concert hall, such as the Victorian tours, behind-the-scenes tours and a tour that includes afternoon tea.

Kensington Gardens were once the private gardens of **Kensington Palace** (www.hrp.org.uk). The palace has been a royal household ever since the asthmatic William of Orange fled damp, polluted Whitehall. A number of monarchs were born here, most recently Victoria in 1819. A number of members of the royal household live in the private side of the palace, with the newest inhabitants being the Duke and Duchess of Cambridge and their three children, Prince George, Princess Charlotte and Prince Louis.

To the north of the gardens is the **Diana, Princess of Wales Memorial Playground** (www.royalparks.org.uk), commemorating the late Princess, who lived at Kensington Palace at the time of her death. A huge wooden Peter Pan-inspired pirate ship on a sandy 'beach', teepees and sensory trails offer hours of fun for children.

KENSINGTON

A few yards from the peace of these parks is busy **Kensington High Street**, which is dominated by chain stores. However, if you take a few steps off this main thoroughfare you will find elegant squares with gorgeous old houses. Situated just next to the neo-Gothic church of St Mary Abbots is **Kensington Church Street**, famed for its antiques shops. At the west end of Kensington High Street is the wooded **Holland Park**, home to a blitzed Jacobean mansion, Holland House, with Japanese gardens and peacocks.

At 18 Stafford Terrace you'll find **Sambourne House**, home of the Victorian Punch illustrator and cartoonist, Linley Sambourne (1844–1910), and just over at 12 Holland Park Road is **Leighton House**, the home of the artist Lord Frederic Leighton from 1866 until he died in 1896 (www.rbkc.gov.uk/museums; charge, ticket for joint admission available). The *pièce de résistance* in Leighton House is the Arab Hall, inspired by a Moorish palace in Palermo. Almost next door is the former Commonwealth Institute, home to the **Design Museum** (https://designmuseum.org; charge for some exhibitions), founded by furniture designer Sir Terence Conran, which presents exhibitions related to architectural, industrial, fashion, graphic and product design. Past displays have explored the work of typeface designer Margaret Calvert, filmmakers Stanley Kubrick and Tim Burton, Ferrari cars and Barbie. The Designer Maker User display on the top floor shows the evolution of design

PORTOBELLO ROAD MARKET

Notting Hill is a gentrified residential area with some of the grandest Georgian townhouses in the capital. The area is also home to the annual Notting Hill Carnival and the Portobello Road Market. Built on the site of a pig farm named after an English victory over Spain at Porto Bello in the Gulf of Mexico in 1739, it has developed over the past 50 years into a major antiques market.

The road accommodates three markets: the antiques market, at the south end, merges into a food market where the traditional fruit-and-vegetable stalls sit alongside more exotic foodstuffs from around the world. A flea market mixing genuine junk with cutting-edge fashion operates under the Westway flyover, at the north end.

from cameras and audio devices to automobiles. Downstairs are temporary galleries and a lecture theatre.

SOUTH KENSINGTON

Familiarly known as 'South Ken', this area is best known for its museums, a legacy of the Great Exhibition of 1851, at which Prince Albert raised money to purchase 87 acres (35 hectares) of land in South Kensington and make this the 'museumland' of London. South Kensington has a large French population, which makes for a number of very good patisseries and some of the best French bookshops in London.

The Natural History Museum

Natural History Museum

On Cromwell Road is the impressive neo-Gothic pile of the **Natural History Museum** ❷ (www.nhm.ac.uk; free except for some special exhibitions), built from 1873–80. The museum's biggest draw is undoubtedly the Dinosaur Gallery – there is also a crowd-pleasing animated model of a Tyrannosaurus Rex, which roars and smells authentically unpleasant. Other highlights include 'Hope', a huge blue whale skeleton suspended from the ceiling in the cathedral-like Hintze Hall and a simulated earthquake in a mock-up of a Japanese supermarket. The Darwin Centre's Cocoon building is a futuristic home for the museum's enormous insect and plant collection.

Science Museum

Next door is the **Science Museum** ❸❸ (www.sciencemuseum.org.uk; free), which traces the history of inventions from the first steam train to the battered command module from the *Apollo 10* space mission. Seven floors of exhibition space cover computing, medicine, photography, chemistry and physics. There are imaginative exhibits on genes and the future of digital communications. The Flight zone houses an IMAX cinema and some flight simulators, while a maths and science interactive gallery offers a giant walk-through model of the solar system and the opportunity to take part in chemistry experiments.

Victoria and Albert Museum

The first director of the **Victoria and Albert Museum** ❸❹ (V&A; Cromwell Road; www.vam.ac.uk; free except for special exhibitions), Henry Cole, began assembling the museum's collection the year after the 1851 Great Exhibition. However, Queen Victoria only laid the foundation stone of the current building in 1899, 38 years after Albert died. Its 1909 facade is by Aston Webb, who also designed the front of Buckingham Palace. Inside is the richest collection of decorative arts in the world, exhibited in beautiful galleries that have been cleverly remodelled to showcase the latest in modern design.

   The collection includes extraordinary groupings of sculpture, pottery, china, engravings, illustrations, metalwork, paintings, textiles, period costumes and furniture. Across seven galleries, the V&A's Photography Centre displays artworks and artefacts tracing photography from its invention to the present day. On the far side of the John Madejski Garden are the spectacular Arts and Crafts-designed Morris, Gamble and Poynter rooms, with their stained glass and Minton tiles. Originally designed as the museum's refreshment rooms, they have been restored to their intended function as a delightful café. Sitting alongside the Henry Cole Wing on Exhibition Road is the grand porticoed Blavatnik Hall,

Victoria and Albert Museum

designed by London-based architect Amanda Levete. It includes the subterranean Sainsbury Gallery for temporary exhibitions and a porcelain-tiled courtyard. The **Young V&A**, tailored towards children, is in Bethnal Green in the East End, and in 2025 a new branch, **V&A East**, will be opening in the Queen Elizabeth Olympic Park.

KNIGHTSBRIDGE

Just south of Hyde Park, Knightsbridge is one of the most expensive chunks of real estate in London and home to **Harrods** ㉟, one of the world's most famous department stores. Opened by Henry Charles Harrod in 1849 as a small grocer's shop, the present terracotta palace – whose facade is lit by some 11,500 light bulbs at night – was built at the turn of the twentieth century. Until 2010, the shop was owned by Mohamed Al Fayed, an Egyptian businessman whose son Dodi

Shopping at Camden Passage

died with Princess Diana in the Paris car crash. Staff claim to be able to source any item you want, and the shop even has a dress code, which security on the door ensure is enforced. The vast Edwardian dining hall – previously home to the department store's famous food halls, but recently refurbished into a culinary hub with restaurants and food bars – is a major attraction, exquisitely decorated with around 1,900 Art Nouveau tiles.

Southwest of Harrods and its more fashionable neighbour, **Harvey Nichols**, is Beauchamp (pronounced 'Beecham') Place. The former village high street is now home to some pricey restaurants and designer shops. **Sloane Street**, a major shopping artery, has back-to-back designer labels and connects Knightsbridge with Chelsea.

CHELSEA

Chelsea has long been at the cutting edge of London fashion. Mary Quant started it with the first boutique (long-gone) on the King's Road, and from the World's End (430 King's Road) avant-garde designer Vivienne Westwood and Malcolm McLaren gave the world punk in the late 1970s. Chelsea in the twenty-first century is more subdued, and the **King's Road** tends nowadays towards chain stores; however, a walk along it is still good for people-watching.

Where Sloane Street meets the King's Road is **Sloane Square** ③⑥, named after Sir Hans Sloane, whose collection formed the basis of the British Museum. Close to the square, the Duke of York's HQ now houses the **Saatchi Gallery** (www.saatchigallery.com; free except special exhibitions). The gallery showcases the work of contemporary artists assembled by former advertising mogul Charles Saatchi, who was an early purchaser of work by one-time YBAs (Young British Artists) such as Tracey Emin's *My Bed* and Damien Hirst's shark in formaldehyde. In 2010 Saatchi announced that he would be gifting the gallery to the nation and in 2019 it became a registered charity – today, it hosts an ever-changing roster of creative art installations and displays by emerging artists.

The **Royal Hospital** on Chelsea Bridge Road, has been a Chelsea landmark since 1692. It is home to the Chelsea Pensioners (retired army veterans), known for their scarlet coats, a design that dates back to the eighteenth century. Between here and the Embankment are Ranelagh Gardens, which host the RHS Chelsea Flower Show (www.rhs.org.uk) every spring. Next to the hospital is the **National Army Museum** (www.nam.ac.uk; free). Continue down to the River Thames along Royal Hospital Road and turn into Tite Street. This attractive residential area is the epitome of bourgeois respectability but in the early nineteenth century it was very bohemian. Look out for the blue plaques on the street dedicated to Oscar Wilde (No 34) and John Singer Sargent (No 31). Turn right on to the Embankment. For garden lovers, take a right down Swan Walk for the **Chelsea Physic Garden** (www.chelseaphysicgarden.co.uk; charge), second only to the one in Oxford as the oldest botanic garden in the country. Back on the Embankment ahead is **Cheyne Walk**. The splendid houses here were on the water's edge until the reclamation of the Embankment in the nineteenth century. Blue plaques mark the former homes of pre-Raphaelite painter Dante Gabriel Rosetti as well as the author George Eliot. Just off Cheyne Walk is **Carlyle's House** (24 Cheyne Row; www.

nationaltrust.org.uk/carlyles-house; charge), home of the Victorian writer, Thomas Carlyle, until his death in 1881.

NORTH LONDON

HIGHLIGHTS
- Islington, see page 88
- Camden, see page 89
- Hampstead and Highgate, see page 89

Easily accessible by Underground, North London has many attractions, including upmarket Hampstead, notable for its heath and literary connections, neighbouring Highgate with its cemetery, and elegant Islington, the stomping ground of the chattering classes. Camden is worth a visit for its busy, bohemian market and its pleasant canal area.

Leafy Cheyne Walk in Chelsea

ISLINGTON

This borough, widely regarded as the territory of well-heeled socialists, symbolises the gentrification of London's Georgian and Victorian dwellings. Classic terraces can be found in areas such as Canonbury Square, where authors George Orwell and Evelyn Waugh once lived. The square is home to the **Estorick Collection** (39a Canonbury Square; www.estorick collection.com; charge), a showcase for modern Italian art housed in a beautiful Georgian building.

The crossroads at the heart of Islington's shopping district is called the Angel, named after a long-gone coaching inn. Adjacent is **Camden Passage**, an upmarket antiques arcade; more affordable bargains can be had at the street market held here on Wednesday and Saturday, with some stalls also on Friday and Sunday (times vary). At the south end of Islington is **Sadler's Wells** (Rosebery Avenue; www.sadlerswells.com), London's top modern dance venue with plenty of events going on throughout the year.

CAMDEN

Markers are the main attraction in **Camden** ㊲. Cheap clothes and souvenir trinkets are sold along Camden High Street, while all kinds of arts, crafts, jewellery, furniture and vintage pieces are on offer at the sprawling **Camden Lock Market**, off Chalk Farm Road (www.camdenlock.net), in and amongst lively street food stalls. Further into the cobbled alleys of the Stables market, you'll find hip designer boutiques, print and vinyl shops, antiques, and more bars and eateries. Camden Lock is on the Regent's Canal, an 8.5-mile (14km) stretch of water running from Paddington to Limehouse in Docklands.

HAMPSTEAD AND HIGHGATE

Exclusive **Hampstead** ㊳ has long been a desirable address, especially among the successful literary set, and it still has its fair share of wealthy celebrity residents. Open spaces predominate. The 3-sq-mile (8-sq-km) **Heath** is the main 'green lung', with Parliament Hill on its south side giving splendid views across London, as does the 112-acre (45-hectare) **Primrose Hill** overlooking Regent's Park to the south.

The elegant **Kenwood House** (Hampstead Lane; www.english-heritage.org.uk/visit/places/kenwood/; free), which overlooks

Hampstead Heath, displays the Iveagh Bequest. The collection includes works by Rembrandt, Reynolds, Turner and Gainsborough.

Sigmund Freud, fleeing the Nazis in 1938, moved from Vienna to Hampstead. The **Freud Museum** (20 Maresfield Gardens; www.freud.org.uk; charge) preserves his house as he left it.

A pretty hilltop suburb, **Highgate** is home to the grandest burial ground in London, **Highgate Cemetery** (Swain's Lane; www.highgatecemetery.org; charge, tours available). There are 170,000 people interred here, including Christina Rossetti, George Eliot and Karl Marx, buried in 53,000 graves.

EAST LONDON

HIGHLIGHTS

- Spitalfields and Whitechapel, see page 90
- Hoxton, see page 92
- Docklands, see page 92
- Stratford, see page 93

This part of London was the first stop for many successive waves of immigrants, whose labour helped to fuel the Industrial Revolution and build the docks through which much of the British Empire's trade passed. Poverty and overcrowding were endemic. Although many areas remain poor, a growing number have now been gentrified and are considered to be quite trendy. Further east still, in Stratford, there has been extensive regeneration, kick-started by the preparations for the London 2012 Olympics.

SPITALFIELDS AND WHITECHAPEL

Just east of Liverpool Street is **Old Spitalfields Market** ❹ (https://oldspitalfieldsmarket.com), a former fruit-and-vegetable market, which has a buzzy bohemian craft, clothing and organic food market. There's an array of excellent international food stalls and a modern shopping arcade with fashion and home stores adjacent.

Nearby is a museum with a difference, the wonderfully atmospheric **Dennis Severs' House** (18 Folgate Street; www.dennissevershouse.co.uk; charge, booking necessary). An American artist, Severs renovated this former eighteenth-century silk-weaver's house in the 1970s, creating a time capsule that assaults the senses – it looks, smells and sounds as if the Huguenots still live there.

Southeast of Spitalfields is **Brick Lane**, known for its proliferation of Indian and Bangladeshi restaurants, street food pop-ups, and indie music and vintage stores. On the northern stretch of Brick Lane there are fashionable boutiques, coffee shops and trendy bars – the latter are mostly within the Old Truman Brewery, the self-styled creative hub of the East End.

Dennis Severs' House

Responding to the East End's spiritual and economic poverty, a local vicar and his wife founded the **Whitechapel Art Gallery** (Whitechapel High Street; www.whitechapelgallery.org; free, charge for select exhibitions) in 1897. The gallery mounts high-profile shows of cutting-edge art and internationally acclaimed artists in a lovely airy space; past exhibitions have included Picasso, Mark Rothko, Frida Kahlo and Ithell Colquhoun. The gallery also hosts performances, live shows and workshops, check online for details. The gallery is open until 9pm every Thursday.

HOXTON

One of the areas in this eastern part of London to experience a huge degree of gentrification is **Hoxton**, near Old Street. The transformation began when artists moved in, many creating studios in redundant warehouses. Art dealers and designers followed, and urban desolation became urban chic. Commercial galleries radiate from **Hoxton Square**. Café-bars and clothes shops line the streets around Curtain Road, and the area is one of London's most popular places for a night out. On Sundays, Hoxton's **Columbia Road Market** specialises in flowers, plants and garden accessories.

DOCKLANDS

In the 1990s, London's docks were transformed. Made derelict by heavy World War II bombing and rendered obsolete by the new container ports to the east, their proximity to the financial institutions of the City made them an attractive location for high-tech office buildings. The 850ft (260m) **Canary Wharf** ㊵ complex, officially called One Canada Square, was the first of several skyscrapers to spring up here. The area is now a lively but somewhat sterile patchwork of huge glass, steel and concrete buildings, with

---

NOTES

An addition to London's public transport network, which coincided with the 2012 Olympic Games, is the IFS Cloud Cable Car (previously the Emirates Air Line). The cable car that runs between North Greenwich (near the O2) over the Thames to the Royal Docks is a great way to get fabulous views of east London, including the Olympic Park and the sweep of the Thames as it heads out to sea. It proved to be an impractical solution for commuters, as first planned, but continues to be a popular attraction for tourists. You can use contactless or your Oyster card at the terminal, or buy a ticket online (discounts available). For more information, check https://tfl.gov.uk/modes/london-cable-car.

a large shopping centre underground. The **Museum of London Docklands** (West India Quay; www.museumoflondon.org.uk/docklands; free) recounts 2,000 years of local history. Highlights include a 20ft (6 metre) model of Old London Bridge and an evocative exhibition about London's role in the slave trade. Past exhibitions and walking tours have covered war-time midwives, medieval markets, Windrush experiences and Black Tudor London. There is a lovely play space for young children – Mudlarks (see website for opening times).

Skyscrapers in Docklands

STRATFORD

One of the strengths of the London 2012 Summer Olympic Games bid was the promise of large-scale redevelopment of some of the capital's most deprived areas, mainly in the east of the city. Once the events were over, the process began of turning the centrepiece of the Games, the Olympic Park in Stratford, into the **Queen Elizabeth Olympic Park** ❹ (www.queenelizabetholympicpark.co.uk). The £292m project involved dismantling the temporary venues – such as the hockey and basketball arenas – and turning the site into an area of parkland, with walking and cycling routes and recreational facilities. Other major venues – the Olympic Stadium, the velodrome and swimming pool – continue to be used for sport. Also open to the public is the 676ft (114.5m) tall ArcelorMittal Orbit (https://arcelormittalorbit.com), the giant twisted sculpture designed by Anish Kapoor and Cecil Balmond, housing the world's longest tunnel slide.

SOUTHEAST LONDON

HIGHLIGHTS
» Greenwich, see page 94
» Dulwich, see page 97

The expansion of the Overground and Jubilee lines into southeast London opened up this area to those who previously dismissed it for being off the main Tube network. There are many riches here, from historic naval Greenwich to artistic Dulwich, with some pretty green spaces, beautiful historic buildings and an exciting food scene.

King George II statue in Grand Square

GREENWICH
Long the favoured destination of nautical and science buffs, **Greenwich** ⓬ enjoyed notoriety in 2000 as the site of the Millennium Dome. The great white tent was built to house a one-year exhibition for the millennium, but was a financial and critical failure. The

structure was later relaunched as the **O2 Arena** (www.theo2.co.uk) and is a popular venue for concerts and sporting events (nearest Tube: North Greenwich).

There are plenty of other reasons to visit villagey Greenwich, not least the number of historic buildings that make up the Maritime Greenwich UNESCO World Heritage Site. The district can be covered in half a day and is at its busiest at weekends, when its thriving centre of craft, antiques and food markets are in full swing. One of the nicest ways to arrive is by boat from Westminster or Tower Bridge, although you can also travel by Docklands Light Railway (DLR) from Bank to Cutty Sark station or by train from London Bridge.

In dry dock on the waterfront is the ***Cutty Sark*** (King William Walk; www.rmg.co.uk/cuttysark; charge), a sailing ship from the great days of the tea-clippers that used to race to be the first to bring the new season's tea from China. The ship reopened to the public in 2012 after it was damaged by a serious fire in 2007. Luckily, at the time of the blaze many of the ship's timbers and its striking figurehead had already been removed to allow restoration work to take place. The ship is set in a huge glass chamber, meaning that you can walk underneath it, touch its hull and even sit underneath it at the café.

Much of the land in the area is taken up by lovely **Greenwich Park** (www.royalparks.org.uk/visit/parks/greenwich-park), at the top of which is Sir Christopher Wren's **Royal Observatory** (www.rmg.co.uk/royal-observatory; charge), where Greenwich Mean Time was established in 1884. It is a steep climb to the Observatory, but the views across to Canary Wharf are splendid and take in many of London's iconic buildings. A brass rule on the ground marks the line between the Eastern and Western hemispheres, making it possible to have a foot in both. Nearby is the South Building, housing the **Planetarium**.

At the base of the park is the imposing **National Maritime Museum** (Romney Road; www.rmg.co.uk/

national-maritime-museum; free except for special exhibitions), which traces the history both of the Royal Navy and the Merchant Navy, as well as the colonisers and discoverers. An extension to the west wing benefits from an attractive broad, glass parkside entrance, four immersive galleries, the AHOY! Children's Gallery (free weekdays in term time) and a pleasant café – however some areas, including AHOY! and the café, are due to be closed until summer 2025 for ongoing roof restoration works, check website for details.

Opposite is the **Old Royal Naval College** (King William Walk; www.ornc.org; charge) designed by Wren, Hawksmoor and Vanbrugh, with gardens by André Le Nôtre. It was built as a hospital for naval pensioners to match Wren's Royal Hospital in Chelsea and was designed in two halves to leave the view free to the river from Inigo Jones' small, but perfectly formed **Queen's House** (Romney Road; www.rmg.co.uk/queens-house; free), a gift to Anne of Denmark from her husband, James. Visitors can enjoy the striking, recently restored Baroque Painted Hall and the art gallery featuring pieces from artists such as L.S. Lowry and Kehinde Wiley, all set in the undercroft along with a café and shop. The area also functions as the main campus for the University of Greenwich.

Dulwich Picture Gallery

The heart of Greenwich lies to the west of the park, where an attractive, old-fashioned **covered market** and neighbouring Greenwich Church Street are lively at weekends.

DULWICH

With its leafy streets, elegant houses and a spacious park, **Dulwich** ㊸ is an oasis of calm. It is largely the creation of one man, Edward Alleyn, an actor-manager who bought land in the area in 1605 and founded an estate to administer a chapel, alms houses and a school for the poor.

> **NOTES**
>
> Just east of Dulwich, in Forest Hill, is the **Horniman Museum** (100 London Road; www.horniman.ac.uk; free except aquarium and butterfly house). Founded in 1901 by Frederick Horniman, a tea merchant, the museum houses rich collections of ethnography and natural history.

The **Dulwich Picture Gallery** (Gallery Road; www.dulwichpicturegallery.org.uk; charge) was formed by combining Alleyn's art collection with a bequest of paintings originally intended for a Polish National Gallery, but diverted when the King of Poland was forced to abdicate. The grand building was designed by Sir John Soane and opened in 1814 as the country's first major public art gallery, with works by masters including Rembrandt, Rubens, Gainsborough and Murillo, and now also hosts exhibitions and talks on subjects from the history of Japanese printmaking to the visionary works of artist Tirzah Garwood, wife of Eric Ravilious.

SOUTHWEST LONDON

HIGHLIGHTS

» Wimbledon, Richmond and Kew, see page 98
» Hampton Court, see page 99

This wealthy area incorporates Wimbledon, synonymous with tennis; genteel Richmond, home to a pleasant shopping centre and a vast area of parkland; Kew, site of the UNESCO-protected Kew Gardens; and Hampton Court, the sixteenth-century riverside palace and favourite residence of Henry VIII.

WIMBLEDON, RICHMOND AND KEW

The suburb of Wimbledon hosts Britain's top tennis tournament in June/July (see page 111), and its history is captured in the **Lawn Tennis Museum** (Church Road, Wimbledon; www.wimbledon.com; charge, tours available). The area is also known for **Wimbledon Common**, a large partly wooded expanse with nature trails.

The main attraction in Richmond is **Richmond Park** (www.royalparks.org.uk/parks/richmond-park), grazed by herds of red and fallow deer and, at 2,350 acres (950 hectares), the largest of the eight royal parks. The original royal residence in the park is the Palladian White Lodge (1727), now used by the Royal Ballet School. **Richmond Green** is the handsome town centre, lined with some fine seventeenth- and eighteenth-century buildings, charming shops and cosy tearooms, and the remains of the twelfth-century royal palace. You can also while away hours at Richmond Riverside, enjoying the lively restaurants on a lazy afternoon, or by walking along the towpath past riverboats and fields, towards a more rural stretch of the Thames.

The nearby suburb of **Kew** ⓮ is synonymous with the **Royal Botanic Gardens** (www.kew.org; charge). The 300-acre (120-hectare) gardens were established in 1759 with the help of Joseph Banks, the botanist who named Botany Bay on Captain James Cook's first voyage to Australia. Other explorers and amateur enthusiasts added their specimens over the centuries, making this a formidable repository and research centre.

The gardens are beautiful, with grand glasshouses including the Palm House, Temperate House, Waterlily House, Princess of Wales Conservatory and Alpine House, and there is an orangery, mock Chinese pagoda, a treetop walkway and the seventeenth-century Dutch House (now known as Kew Palace), a former royal palace where George III was locked up when it was thought that he had gone mad. You could really spend a whole day here, making use the themed trail maps provided by the park. More recent additions include The Hive, a multi-sensory installation showing the role of bees in the food chain and the dangers to their population, and a Children's Garden, featuring a 4m (13ft) high canopy walk and educational zones exploring everything that a plant needs to grow.

Hampton Court Palace

HAMPTON COURT

Located 14 miles (23km) west of central London and easily accessible by train from Waterloo or by riverboat from Westminster or Richmond, the Tudor **Hampton Court Palace** ㊺ (www.hrp.org.uk/hampton-court-palace; charge) was built in 1514 for Cardinal Wolsey but appropriated by Henry VIII in 1525, following Wolsey's fall from grace. Surrounded by 60 acres (24 hectares) of immaculate riverside gardens, it was Henry's favourite palace – he spent five of his six honeymoons here. Although the State Apartments are sumptuous, featuring works by such gifted craftsmen as Antonio Verrio and William Kent, the highlights of the visit are the Great Hall and Chapel Royal. Also popular is the 300-year-old palace maze.

Carnaby Street lights up for Christmas

Things to do

London has some of the greatest theatres in the world and is at the cutting edge of fashion, music and the arts. For up-to-the-minute entertainment listings consult the weekly events magazine *Time Out* (www.timeout.com/london) or the newspapers *Metro* (www.metro.co.uk) and *The Evening Standard* (www.standard.co.uk), all three free and available at tube and train stations as well as online. The weekend newspapers usually also include a listings guide – *The Guide*, which comes with Saturday's *Guardian*, is pretty comprehensive.

SHOPPING

With more than 30,000 shops, London is a year-round shopping destination, and it is no surprise that people flock here from all over the world for some retail therapy. However specialised your retail needs, you can be sure that somewhere in this sprawling city there is a shop that can meet them.

SHOPPING STREETS AND DISTRICTS

While the size of the city makes it impossible to cover it in a week, from a shopper's point of view London is relatively easy to navigate. The city is loosely divided into shopping districts, each offering its own experience. The underground is usually the quickest means of getting from area to area, while the bus system is excellent but less easy to navigate. Distances between some streets, such as Oxford Street, Tottenham Court Road, Regent Street and Bond Street, are short enough to walk.

Oxford Street is the capital's main shopping thoroughfare, packed from end to end with hundreds of stores. West of Oxford Circus are some large department stores, including upmarket Selfridges, John Lewis and Marks & Spencer. All the main high-street chains have shops here, including enormous flagship branches of ZARA, Adidas and Nike (near Oxford Circus) and Primark (near Marble Arch).

Battersea Power Station

The shops on **Regent Street** range from upmarket high-street chains such as All Saints, Anthropologie, COS, Reiss and & Other Stories to designer brands including Burberry and Tommy Hilfiger. It is home to Hamleys (Britain's largest toy shop), the Apple Store and the London institution Liberty.

Tottenham Court Road is dominated by electronics and home stores such as West Elm. **Charing Cross Road**, which runs all the way down to Trafalgar Square, is sadly no longer the preserve of second-hand and antiquarian bookshops it once was but is still home to the seven-floor Foyles bookshop.

Covent Garden is one of London's most popular retail areas, with shops ranging from high-street and cutting-edge fashion boutiques to quirky specialists selling everything from teapots to kites. Although **Soho** has never quite lost its seedy image, between the sex shops are some fine delicatessens, art shops and some great fashion boutiques selling hip urbanwear.

In the Piccadilly area (the southern end of Regent Street), you'll find the upmarket grocer's **Fortnum & Mason**, notable for its gorgeous window displays, the flagship **Waterstones**, the largest bookshop in Europe, as well as some swanky cafés and some of London's oldest shops, many of which hold royal warrants to supply the royal family with goods. Nearby **Jermyn Street** specialises in menswear. **Old Bond Street** and **New Bond Street**, in Mayfair, offer a vast choice of designer labels. Savile Row, again in Mayfair, specialises in bespoke tailoring, and Cork Street, with its numerous galleries, is an art-lover's dream.

Even in the mainstream West End there are unusual enclaves lined with boutiques and galleries, such as **St Christopher's Place**. On villagey **Marylebone High Street**, gourmet food shops jostle with upmarket boutiques and several stylish homeware stores, including the branch of the Conran Shop that sparked regeneration along this strip.

The City has its very own shopping centre, One New Change, which offers stunning views of St Paul's Cathedral from its sixth floor terrace (terrace closed for construction work at the time of writing).

For those wanting the best of European and international designer fashions, **Knightsbridge**, home to the high-class department stores Harrods and Harvey Nichols, has the highest concentration of such shops. Haute couture names from Armani to Yves Saint Laurent sit next to established British designers.

Although the **King's Road** is no longer as trendy as in its sixties heyday, shoppers still flock to it for its concentration of upmarket chain stores and small boutiques on Sloane Square. In nearby **Belgravia**, there's a fleet of sleek designer shops, swanky restaurants and fancy bakeries, spread across the pretty Georgian buildings of areas including Pimlico Road, with Newson's Yard opening in late 2023, Elizabeth Street and open-air Eccleston Yards. **Kensington Church Street** is a favourite destination for antiques lovers. **Notting Hill**, home of Portobello market, also has many fashionable boutiques, upmarket chains and colourful independents.

Further west, **Shepherd's Bush** is one of London's busiest shopping destinations since the opening of **Westfield London**. Far to the east, by the Queen Elizabeth Olympic Park, is another vast shopping centre, Westfield Stratford City.

Columbia Road Flower Market

Down by the river, after standing derelict for years, the iconic Art Deco **Battersea Power Station** reopened to the public in 2022, redesigned as an immense retail and leisure complex. The Grade II listed building was a working power station between 1930–80, and after a monster transformation it now houses a slew of high street and higher-end designer shops, a food hall, the luxury *art'otel* with rooftop swimming pool, and a chimney lift for river views.

MARKETS

London has markets to suit all tastes. Daily, historic covered **Old Spitalfields**, near Liverpool Street, is a great and bustling place to spot up-and-coming talent, as fashion and accessory designers run many of the stalls. The market is renowned for its food stalls, too, showcasing an array of international cuisines. On Sunday, nearby cobbled **Columbia Road** is busy with stalls selling every type of cut flower and houseplant imaginable; this fashionable area is also dotted with independent boutiques selling hip fashions, homewares and gourmet organic produce.

With eight heaving indoor and outdoor markets, **Camden** is the place to go for arts and crafts, furnishings and alternative fashion. In the west, iconic, colourful **Portobello Road** is renowned for its antiques but also sells fashions, food and bric-a-brac – Saturday morning is the best time to go.

Further south, the fabulous Market Halls put Victoria on the foodie map in 2018, with three glorious floors of permanent stalls including the popular *Egglsut*, selling their famous egg sandwiches; delicious Malaysian food at *Gopal's Corner*, a spin-off from cult favourite *Roti King*; and *Butchies*, the East London-born fried buttermilk chicken shop.

South of the river, trendy **Borough Market** is a foodie heaven, with stalls ranging from the Spanish *Brindisa* and Lebanese *Arabica* to the resolutely British *Ginger Pig* and *Kappacasein* (a cheese lover's heaven), to fresh fish stalls and organic grocers. Vibrant **Brixton**, meanwhile, is home to a medley of excellent, vibrant markets featuring street food from around the world.

CULTURE

Whether you are after theatre, opera, clubs or pubs, there is no shortage of entertainment in London.

THEATRE

London's theatrical history goes back to a playhouse opened at Shoreditch in 1576 by James Burbage, son of a carpenter and travelling player. Nowadays, London's theatres – staging comedies, musicals and dramas – are concentrated in the **West End**. To buy discounted same-day tickets for West End shows, visit the 'TKTS' booth in Leicester Square, or online at www.officiallondontheatre.com.

Other theatres include the **National Theatre** at the Southbank Centre (see page 63; www.nationaltheatre.org.uk), which stages innovative productions of the classics, some excellent modern pieces and the occasional rousing musical revival. The **Old Vic** (see page 63; www.oldvictheatre.com) specialises in revivals of the classics, while the nearby **Young Vic** (see page 63; www.youngvic.org) leans towards more recent, experimental theatre. Chelsea's **Royal Court Theatre** (Sloane Square; www.royalcourttheatre.com) is famous for cutting-edge drama, and the buzzy bar and kitchen downstairs is a lovely place for a bite to eat or a drink, whether you are watching a show or not. **Shakespeare's Globe** (see page 66; www.shakespearesglobe.com), on Bankside, stages works by the Bard and his contemporaries. East along the river by Tower Bridge, the Bridge Theatre (www.bridgetheatre.co.uk), founded in 2017, is a venture from Nicholas Hytner and Nick Starr, of National Theatre fame.

In addition to the West End theatres there are dozens of fine suburban playhouses and multiple fringe venues, championing new, experimental works. In summer outdoor theatre is popular, too, in venues such as **Regent's Park** (www.openairtheatre.com).

Musical theatre continues to be enormously popular, and the quality is generally high. Some shows are fairly permanently based at their theatres, such as the longest-running musical in the West End, *Les Misérables* at the **Sondheim Theatre** (51 Shaftesbury Avenue; www.lesmis.com), and Andrew Lloyd Webber's gothic masterpiece, *Phantom of the Opera* at **Her Majesty's Theatre** (Haymarket; tel: www.thephantomoftheopera.com). Other shows and exports from Broadway, like *Mamma Mia!* at the **Novello Theatre** (Aldwych; www.mamma-mia.com) and *Wicked* at the **Apollo Victoria** (17 Wilton Road; www.wickedthemusical.co.uk), have also made their mark.

MUSIC, OPERA AND BALLET

Top concert venues include the **Royal Festival Hall** (see page 62; www.southbankcentre.co.uk), with its improved acoustics, and the **Barbican** (see page 74; www.barbican.org.uk, www.lso.co.uk), home of the London Symphony Orchestra; the **Royal Albert Hall** (see page 81; www.royalalberthall.com) hosts the summer BBC Promenade Concerts (the 'Proms'), while the **Wigmore Hall** (see page 59; www.wigmore-hall.org.uk) does chamber recitals. Lunchtime concerts are held in churches including Westminster's St John's, Smith Square, which merged with Southbank Sinfonia to become **Sinfonia Smith Square** (www.sinfoniasmithsq.org.uk)

in 2024, **St Martin-in-the-Fields** (see page 35; www.stmartin-in-the-fields.org) and Piccadilly's **St James's** (see page 52; www.sjp.org.uk).

London's main venues for opera and ballet are Covent Garden's **Royal Ballet and Opera** (see page 46; www.rbo.org.uk) and the **Coliseum**, commonly called the **ENO** (www.eno.org), as it's the home of the English National Opera (performances in English), in St Martin's Lane. For modern dance, try the capital's leading venue, **Sadler's Wells Theatre** (see page 89; www.sadlerswells.com).

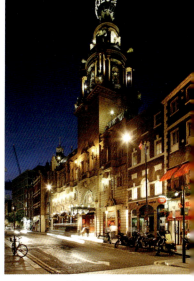

The London Coliseum

Jazz venues include **Ronnie Scott's** (47 Frith Street; www.ronniescotts.co.uk), **Jazz Café** (5 Parkway, Camden; www.thejazzcafelondon.com) and the **Pizza Express Jazz Club Soho** (10 Dean Street; www.pizzaexpresslive.com).

London is one of the best places to catch live music in any number of contemporary genres. The big-name venue is **The O2** (Peninsula Square, Greenwich; www.theo2.co.uk), a 20,000-capacity arena housed in the former Millennium Dome. Other popular venues include the Art Deco **O2 Academy Brixton** (211 Stockwell Road) and the more intimate **O2 Shepherd's Bush Empire** (Shepherd's Bush Green; for both venues www.academymusicgroup.com), or the **Roundhouse** (Chalk Farm Road, Camden; www.roundhouse.org.uk).

Heading out for a night on the town in Soho

NIGHTLIFE

London is a great place to party, with hundreds of bars and clubs offering an eclectic range of music to a diverse clientele. Soho has long been central to London's mainstream nightlife, and still has plenty of great bars, and there are a few reliable pubs around Leicester Square. Try **Bar Soho** (23–25 Old Compton Street; www.barsoho.co.uk), a fun spot in the thick of the action; unpretentious, lively cocktail bar **Be at One** (17 Greek Street; www.beatone.co.uk), whisky bar **Milroy's** (3 Greek Street; www.milroysofsoho.com) and **Swift** (12 Old Compton Street; www.barswift.com), a split-level cocktail bar with a buzzy crowd upstairs and a speakeasy-style lounge on the floor below. **Cahoots** (13 Kingly Street; www.cahoots.co.uk) is a vintage-Tube-themed bar, complete with sandbags, classic signs and an old Tube carriage, and another fun option down towards Piccadilly is the gloriously Art Deco **Bar Américain** (22 Sherwood Street; www.brasseriezedel.com) at the grand French *Brasserie Zédel*.

Shoreditch and Hoxton (near Old Street tube station) draw trendy crowds. Popular **93 Feet East** (Truman Brewery, 150 Brick Lane; www.93feeteast.co.uk) has a relaxed vibe with music ranging from indie to hip-hop to retro; while **333 Mother** (333 Old Street; www.333oldstreet.com) is a Hoxton stalwart offering highly eclectic music. You'll find live music and an electric atmosphere at **Blues**

Kitchen (134–146 Curtain Road; www.theblueskitchen.com) offering live blues, soul and jazz, and **Old Street Records** (350–356 Old Street; www.oldstreetrecords.com) a fun, moodily-lit, industrial-looking bar good for cocktails and dancing.

The rich, royal, famous and upwardly mobile like to party in the exclusive clubs of Mayfair and Kensington. There are many seriously swanky joints to choose from if you're up for some elite clubbing, and it's good to plan ahead as entry can be strict, but the theatrical **Cirque le Soir** (15–21 Ganton Street; www.cirquelesoir.com) is a favourite haunt.

Camden is the place to go for indie and rock music, with gorgeous, recently renovated **KOKO** (1a Camden High Street; www.koko.co.uk), sweaty basement venue **The Underworld** (174 Camden High Street; www.theunderworldcamden.co.uk) and the iconic **Electric Ballroom** (184 Camden High Street; www.electricballroom.co.uk) leading the way.

Brixton has a range of partying options as diverse as the area itself, including the **Dogstar** (www.dogstarbrixton.com), a dance bar at 389 Coldharbour Lane, **The Prince of Wales** (467-469 Brixton Road) with a rooftop terrace and the leading heavyweight **Electric Brixton** (Town Hall Parade; www.electricbrixton.uk.com) with live DJ sets.

Dotted across town, superclubs such as **Fabric** (77a Charterhouse Street, Farringdon; www.fabriclondon.com) and **Ministry of Sound** (103 Gaunt Street, Elephant and Castle; www.ministryofsound.com) attract top international DJs.

For the LGBTQI+ scene, Soho, Vauxhall and the East End are your best bet, with endless bars and diverse clubs ranging from **Heaven** (The Arches, Villiers Street, Charing Cross; www.g-a-yandheaven.co.uk), home to the legendary G-A-Y club nights, to **Fire** (South Lambeth Road, Vauxhall; www.firelondon.net), serving up house and electro beats and the thriving **Dalston Superstore** (117 Kingsland High Street; www.dalstonsuperstore.com), the the LGBTQI+ heart of the East End.

Most clubs don't get going until midnight; some run all night. The Night Tube has made getting home easier for clubbers, although this only runs on Fridays and Saturday nights. On other days, your only options are an expensive taxi or a night bus.

OUTDOOR ACTIVITIES

London offers horse riding and boating in Hyde Park, pedalo rides in Regent's Park, swimming at Hampstead Heath, rowing on the Thames, and cycling pretty much all over.

The **football** season runs from August to May, with matches usually held on Saturday and Sunday afternoons. The top London clubs are: Arsenal (Emirates Stadium; www.arsenal.com), Chelsea (Stamford Bridge; www.chelseafc.com) and Tottenham Hotspur (White Hart Lane; www.tottenhamhotspur.com). Wembley Stadium (www.wembleystadium.com) hosts the FA Cup final and national games. **Rugby** is played from September to April/May. Major Rugby Union games are played at Twickenham (www.allianz stadiumtwickenham.com). **Cricket** is played in summer at the Oval (Kennington, SE11; www.kiaoval.com) and Lord's (St John's Wood, www.lords.org).

QUEEN ELIZABETH OLYMPIC PARK

In July 2005, London surprised itself by winning its bid to host the 2012 Olympic Games, which saw long-neglected parts of east London transformed to house the main stadia and Olympic Village. It was set amidst newly created parkland in Stratford and included the Olympic Stadium, Aquatics Centre, Velopark and Basketball Arena. Today, the park hosts major sporting events, from basketball to football and track cycling, as well as numerous art and culture attractions and parkland trails. In 2022, the park also became the exclusive home to the revolutionary virtual ABBA Voyage concerts, shown in a specially built arena. In 2025, the park will also be the home of the new V&A East Museum.

Wimbledon is the venue for the famous two-week annual tennis championship in June/July. Seats for Centre Court and Courts 1 and 2 should be reserved six months in advance. However, you can queue on the day for outside court tickets, and you may be able to buy cheap returns in the afternoon. For information contact the All England Lawn Tennis Club (www.wimbledon.com).

One of London's most famous sporting events is the Easter **University Boat Race**, during which rowers from Oxford and Cambridge universities race along the Thames from Putney to Mortlake. The **London Marathon** in April attracts the top athletes from around the world, as well as roughly 50,000 other runners.

Diana Memorial Fountain

CHILDREN

London's parks and attractions guarantee youngsters a fun time. The Diana, Princess of Wales' Playground, in Kensington Gardens, has a huge wooden pirate ship and wonderful Peter Pan-inspired playground. In nearby Hyde Park is the Diana, Princess of Wales' Memorial Fountain, where kids can dip their toes in. Animal-loving kids will enjoy a visit to **London Zoo** (see page 58) or the **Sea Life London Aquarium** (see page 61; look out for 2-for-1 offers with train tickets), while celebrity-spotters should visit **Madame Tussauds** (see page 59).

Children can clamber over the old buses and trams and play on pretend vehicles at the **London Transport Museum** (see page 47), while the **Natural History Museum** (see page 83) is home to the ever-popular robotic T-Rex. The **Science Museum** (see page 84) has the interactive Garden play space in the basement plus the Fly Zone with simulators. The **Tower of London** (see page 77) enlivens history thanks to Beefeaters with traditional costumes and stories to tell.

London has two toy museums. The **Young V&A** (Cambridge Heath Road; www.vam.ac.uk/young; free) in **Bethnal Green** is the largest public collection of dolls' houses, games and puppets on view in the world and has plenty of space for little children to roam.

For toys to take home as gifts, shop at the vast **Hamleys** in Regent Street. **Harrods** is also fun for children. A ride on the **London Eye** (see page 62) is an exciting half an hour for older children.

FESTIVALS AND EVENTS

January New Year's Day Parade.

January/February Chinese New Year: celebrations in Soho's Chinatown and Trafalgar Square, including traditional lion dances and a parade.

March/April Oxford versus Cambridge University Boat Race: the mighty institutions battle it out on the Thames.

April London Marathon: the world's largest marathon, with over 50,000 runners raising huge sums for charity.

May Chelsea Flower Show (third or fourth week): the most prestigious annual gardening exhibition in the world.

June Trooping the Colour (Sat nearest June 11): the monarch inspects the troops at the parade for the official birthday of the British sovereign. The Wimbledon Championships (late June/early July): the world's greatest tennis players compete at the All England Lawn Tennis Club.

Late June/early July Pride in London: Huge annual street party with music, films, performances and cultural events in celebration of the LGBTQI+ community.

July–September Henry Wood Promenade Concerts, known as the 'Proms': classical concerts for eight weeks at the Royal Albert Hall.

August Notting Hill Carnival: huge street party around Ladbroke Grove and Portobello Road.

September Great River Race (Sat in early to mid-Sept): hundreds of traditional boats race from Docklands to Richmond, also known as the London River Marathon.

October Trafalgar Day Parade (Sun nearest Oct 21): celebrates Lord Nelson's sea victory over Napoleon. The BFI London Film Festival and London Literature Festival also run for two weeks mid-October around the Southbank.

November State Opening of Parliament (month can vary due to general election dates): watch the monarch and royal procession en route to mark the start of a new parliamentary session. Lord Mayor's Show (second Sat): a popular pageant of carnival floats and the newly elected Lord Mayor in procession from the Guildhall to the Law Courts. Guy Fawkes' Day (Nov 5): fireworks displays and bonfires across the city, commemorating the failed attempt to blow up Parliament. Christmas lights switched on in Oxford and Regent streets.

December Christmas markets pop up around London. New Year's Eve: spectacular fireworks display by the Thames.

Notting Hill Carnival

Food and drink

London's food scene – host to a colourful riot of restaurants, pop-ups, food markets, cafés and pubs, and an array of culinary innovators celebrating gastronomy from all over the globe – has earned the city a reputation as one of the foodie capitals of the world. The city boasts around 12,000 restaurants, covering every cuisine imaginable – a reflection of its diverse population and draw as an international destination. At the top end there are some world-class restaurants, and prices can be wildly expensive, but there are also some affordable, good value places to eat offering quality cuisine.

Not long ago, British food had a bad reputation. Lack of imagination, lack of taste and overcooked vegetables were often cited, and the cuisine was internationally derided, with the French President Jacques Chirac famously saying 'you can't trust people who cook as badly as that'. But the last few decades have seen a remarkable transformation. A resurgence of interest in locally-grown produce and high-quality, organic ingredients mean that foods such as Cromer crab, Cornish sprats, Gressingham duck, Herdwick lamb or Galloway beef are familiar features on the British menu, and more establishments are working with vegetables grown locally in their own kitchen gardens.

The rebirth of British cuisine was somewhat characterized by a new generation of chefs, many of whom inspired innovative approaches to cooking and sought to provide elevated dining experiences, became household names with popular TV shows and achieved celebrity status. The outspoken chef Gordon Ramsay was one of the first of several London-based restaurateurs who raised expectations of what should be on offer, garnering Michelin stars along the way. As can be expected, London's higher-end destination restaurants often need reserving well in advance.

This culinary zeal filtered down to more modest restaurants and even the local pub. A major component of the city's social history,

WHERE TO EAT

London has around 3500 pubs. Several of these date from as long ago as the seventeenth century, and many retain the atmosphere of that era with open fireplaces and traditional oak-panelled walls. Encouraged by the 2007 smoking ban, many pubs concentrated on food as much as drinks, serving updated versions of traditional 'pub grub', such as bangers and mash, a Ploughman's lunch, steak and kidney pie and the traditional Sunday roast. 'Gastropubs' – light, airy, fashionably furnished bars that serve a more adventurous range of dishes – are peppered across almost all areas of the capital.

These days, in addition to the established British classics, you'll find restaurants all over London offering food from around the world, many at least experimenting with internationally influenced flavours. 'Fusion cuisine' in particular is increasingly popular, with places offering dishes that blend elements of, say, Chinese and Indian, or Polish and Mexican (see page 125). Many eateries are also keen to provide interesting, aesthetically tuned dining experiences, serving carefully curated plates with visual, photo-worthy (and perhaps social-media worthy) appeal.

Dinner at St. John

WHERE TO EAT

The main concentration of restaurants is in the West End, with the biggest variety in the frenetic streets of Soho – a high-energy hub of beloved long-standing

EATING AND DRINKING HOURS

In general, breakfast is served 7–noon, lunch from noon–3pm, afternoon tea 3–5pm, and dinner 6–11pm. In practice, you can eat whatever you want, whenever you want – Soho and Covent Garden have the most options for round-the-clock dining. Most pubs are only open Mon–Sat 11am–11pm (though many stay open a couple of hours later on Fri and Sat) and Sun noon–10.30pm. Many restaurants close earlier on Sunday evenings, so check online beforehand.

institutions side-by-side with the newest hotspots. While many chain restaurants aimed at theatregoers in Covent Garden offer good-value, pre-show deals, the area has become a fine-dining enclave, home to big-hitters such as *The Barbary* (see page 124). Upmarket Kensington, Chelsea and Notting Hill are home to numerous designer restaurants, while the City has many similarly stylish haunts like oyster bars and big-budget restaurants, aimed at the business luncher, and East London offers a combination of hip eateries across all budgets, including Spitalfields market and a concentration of Indian and Bangladeshi restaurants. King's Cross is home to a cluster of restaurants, including those around the recently refurbished buildings of Coal Drops Yard and Granary Square. Popular, bustling food markets are dotted all over (see page 119). Further out from the centre, you'll find newer crops of foodie hubs thriving in areas both north and south of the river, from Hackney and Stoke Newington to Greenwich and Peckham.

TOP 10 THINGS TO TRY

1. FULL ENGLISH BREAKFAST

This hearty meal, also known as a 'fry up', consists of fried eggs, bacon, sausage, tomatoes, beans, mushrooms, black pudding and toast, served with a cup of tea or coffee. For a cheaper option, head

TOP 10 THINGS TO TRY 117

to one of London's caffs known as 'greasy spoons', such as *E Pellici* in Bethnal Green (www.epellicci.co.uk), or for a grander breakfast experience treat yourself to 'The English' at *The Wolseley* in Mayfair (see page 126).

2. AFTERNOON TEA

This quintessentially British event traditionally takes place in some of the high-end hotels and fashionable department stores, and consists of sandwiches, scones with cream and jam, a variety of cakes and a pot of tea. The brew varies from classic Indian teas such as Assam and Darjeeling to the more flowery Earl Grey. Classic venues include *Claridge's* (Brook Street, W1; www.claridges.co.uk), *The Ritz* (see page 53) and *Fortnum & Mason* (see page 125). Many places are renowned for more artistic afternoon tea experiences, such as the quirky Gallery at *Sketch* (9 Conduit Street, W1; https://sketch.london).

Afternoon tea at The Ritz

3. SUNDAY ROAST

The Sunday roast remains one of the UK's favourite dishes. You can expect a choice of roasted meats, including beef, lamb, pork or chicken, served with a Yorkshire pudding and a selection of vegetables and roast potatoes, accompanied by gravy and other condiments such as horseradish sauce, mint sauce or mustard. You'll find a roast on the menu of many restaurants and almost every pub, and pretty much everywhere offers a vegetarian option, such as a veggie wellington.

4. FISH AND CHIPS

The humble fish and chips is a British staple – tuck into flaky fish in a crispy golden batter, served with chunky chips and doused in salt and vinegar, often with a side of mushy peas. Look for traditional takeaways that serve them wrapped in newspaper, or go for a sit-down affair at *Rock & Sole Plaice* in Covent Garden (47 Endell Street; www.rockandsoleplaice.com), *Golden Hind* in Marylebone (71a–73 Marylebone Lane; www.goldenhindrestaurant.com) or *Poppies* in the East End (6–8 Hanbury Street; www.poppiesfishandchips.co.uk).

5. PIE AND MASH

For a taste of the old East End look for a pie and mash shop, where you'll get minced beef pie and mashed potatoes with gravy or a green parsley sauce – a meal that has been popular among the working class and Cockneys for centuries. Originally the pies were filled with eels, but now they are more likely to be filled with beef or vegetables and sometimes served with a side of jellied eels instead. Try *Manze's* (87 Tower Bridge Road; www.manze.co.uk) or *Goddards at Greenwich* in the South East (22 King William Walk; www.goddardsatgreenwich.co.uk).

6. LONDON PUBS

Traditional, centuries-old taphouses, charming riverside haunts with picturesque views, or tucked-away hidden gems – London's pub scene is hard to beat. Many of London's historic drinking houses have survived fires, been the setting for famous films, or otherwise have interesting stories to tell. Try the galleried *George Inn* at London Bridge (75 Borough High Street), the historic *Lamb and Flag* in Covent Garden (33 Rose Street), once renowned for its bare-knuckle fights, the cosy *Bricklayer's Arms* just off Tottenham

Court Road (31 Gresse Street) or the spy-themed *Morpeth Arms* (58 Millbank), with views of the Lego-like MI6 building over the river.

7. PUDDINGS

It's easy to find sweet treats and desserts all over London, and it's traditional to round off a meal with something sugary. Visitors may want to try British classics like trifle, jam roly-poly, rhubarb or apple crumble smothered in sweet, hot, vanilla- flavoured custard, or Eton mess – but nothing quite beats the sticky toffee pudding, a dark date sponge cake drizzled with warm toffee sauce and served with a scoop of ice cream.

Lamb & Flag in Covent Garden

8. FOOD MARKETS

One thing London is famed for is its array of food markets, food halls and street-food pop-ups. These foodie destinations are on the rise, and you can while away hours at one of them, sampling all kinds of tasty cuisine. Try the sprawling Borough Market in Southwark; bustling Broadway Market in Hackney; cool Mercato Metropolitano in Elephant and Castle; trendy Camden Market; the delightful street-food stalls by the Southbank; the vast, glassy Arcade Food Hall by Tottenham Court Road station, or any of the buzzy, multi-level Market Halls in Victoria, Canary Wharf and Oxford Street (with a new one due to open in Paddington in 2025).

9. INTERNATIONAL CUISINE

London is home to some of the finest international restaurants in the world. One of the best things about eating out here is the incredible variety of cuisines on offer and the chance to experience a rich array of culinary traditions. London's status as an international city attracts chefs from every country and culture, so from French, Italian and Spanish to Nigerian, Gambian, Afghan, Lebanese, Turkish, Mexican, Thai, Vietnamese, Chinese and Indian – you're spoilt for choice.

10. CHEESE

The Brits love cheese, and the UK produces some very fine specimens, on a par even with those from France or Italy. No matter what kind of cheese you like – soft, hard, mature, mild, artisan, farmhouse, blue or otherwise – London is full to the brim of shops to suit any cheese-lover's taste, and they often offer free samples at the counter. Places to shop include the long-standing Paxton & Whitfield, Neal's Yard Dairy, Leadenhall Market and various stalls at Borough Market.

Curries in Camden Market

WHAT TO DRINK

Beer in the UK comes in various forms, from lager (the most popular) to ale (brewed using only top-fermenting yeasts; sweeter and fuller bodied) to stout (creamy, almost coffee-like beer made from roasted malts or roast barley), of which the most famous brand is probably Guinness (and in exciting news for fans of the Irish tipple, a Guinness microbrewery is set to open in Covent Garden in 2025).

Pubs generally serve beer either 'draught' or from the cask. In the case of the former, a keg is pressurised with carbon-dioxide gas, which drives the beer to the dispensing tap. For the latter, beer is pulled from the cask via a beer line with a hand pump at the bar. This method is generally used for what is often termed 'real ale': unfiltered and unpasteurised beer. A slew of independent taprooms and small craft breweries have opened in recent years, with many offering brewery tours and tastings of London craft beers and house ales. Most places now offer a few **non-alcoholic** or **low-alcohol** beer options, too, as well as the usual fare of **soft drinks** and juices.

Every pub or restaurant will have a wide, international selection of **wine** available, with reds, whites and rosés on most menus. English wines, especially sparkling, are becoming more popular, made with grapes grown in wineries in the countryside – Kent-produced Chapel Down and Sussex-produced Nyetimber are worth looking out for. In recent years, more people have been seeking out natural or low-intervention wines, which are featured on many wine lists. London has also seen a rise of urban wineries and is now home to four of them, including the cutting-edge Renegade Urban Winery in Walthamstow (www.renegadelondonwine.com).

A longer-established English tipple is **cider**, made from the fermented juice of apples and produced predominantly in the Southwest since before the Romans arrived. Pubs usually offer a choice of cider from a tap or bottles of sweet, fruity options.

Another speciality is **whisky**, produced in Scotland and Ireland. Most pubs in central London will offer a small selection of both, and there are a few dedicated whisky bars around, though aficionados may consider joining the Whisky Society, which has its tasting events at 19 Greville Street in Hatton Garden, Clerkenwell (www.smws.co.uk).

Places to eat

We have used the following symbols to give an idea of the price for a two-course meal for one, including wine and service:

££££ = £55 and over
£££ = £35–55
££ = £25–35
£ = below £25

WESTMINSTER

Cinnamon Club 30–2 Great Smith Street, SW1, www.cinnamonclub.com. Excellent, innovative Indian fine dining with a signature tasting menu, located in the historic Grade II listed building that housed the Old Westminster Library. **£££**

Gordon's Wine Bar 47 Villiers Street, WC2, www.gordonswinebar.com. Located just north of Embankment tube is this favourite London watering hole, where drinkers sit under the arches on chilly nights and out on the terrace in summer. Sherry and port are specialities here. They don't take reservations, and it can get busy, so arrive early for a table. **££**

The Port House 417 Strand, WC2, www.theporthouse.co.uk. You could almost miss this tiny, candlelit tapas restaurant on the Strand, but it's worth seeking out. An extensive menu offers Spanish delights – try the gambas (prawns) or txistorras (chorizo sausages) – and a choice of ports, wines and sherries in an ambient setting. **££**

The Portrait National Portrait Gallery, St Martin's Place, WC2, www.theportraitrestaurant.com. When it comes to location, few can beat the National Portrait Gallery's top-floor restaurant with its wonderful views of Trafalgar Square, Big Ben and the London Eye. Above-average gallery food on a carefully curated, seasonal menu, and a good-value pre-theatre deal. **£££**

SOHO AND CHINATOWN

Andrew Edmunds 46 Lexington Street, W1, www.andrewedmunds.com. A lack of signage out front gives a secretive feel to this cosy old-Soho hideaway, located in an eighteenth-century townhouse. Inside, the wood-panelled walls are lit by candlelight and dishes are modern European, ranging from semolina gnocchi to smoked ox tongue. **£££**

Bar Italia 22 Frith Street, W1, www.baritaliasoho.co.uk. Retaining its genuine 1950s feel, this is London's most famous Italian bar. No hype, just excellent coffee and a cosmopolitan crowd. Stays open through the night (sometimes to 3 or 4am). **£**

Berenjak 27 Romily St, W1, www.berenjaklondon.com. Since opening in 2018, Berenjak has become a foodie favourite, offering high-end, traditional Persian cuisine, from charcoal-grilled kababs to fragrant aubergine stews with piping-hot flatbread. There's another branch in Borough. **£££**

Bocca di Lupo 12 Archer Street, W1, www.boccadilupo.com. Buzzy Italian restaurant serving a range of regional dishes such as risotto of Italian prawns and roast suckling pig. **£££**

Dean Street Townhouse 69–71 Dean Street, W1, www.sohohouse.com. The restaurant of this stylish Soho hotel manages to combine the style of a French brasserie with the delights of simple English food – the fish and chips are particularly good. **££££**

Kiln 58 Brewer Street, W1, www.kilnsoho.com. One of the best places to eat in the thick of Soho, this small, joyfully noisy open-fire restaurant serves delicious Thai-inspired food, from clay pot glass noodles with crab meat to grilled soy chicken or smoked kippers with lemongrass salad. **££**

Randall & Aubin 16 Brewer Street, W1, www.randallandaubin.com. Named after the old delicatessen that inhabited this spot from 1904 to the late 1990s, *Randall & Aubin* is a buzzy, romantic place doing champagne, seafood and succulent roasts. Piles of lobster, crab and oysters greet you as you enter, the music is frenetic and the tables close to each other. Also does classic French and British dishes. **£££**

Speedboat Bar 30 Rupert Street, W1, www.speedboatbar.co.uk. Inspired by Bangkok's Chinatown, this is a fun place to eat, serving fiery and fragrant Thai dishes from crispy black-pepper pork to pickled mustard greens in vibrant, retro style surroundings. **££**

COVENT GARDEN

Ave Mario 15 Henrietta Street, WC2, www.bigmammagroup.com. Joyful Italian restaurant in the heart of Covent Garden with cool, quirky décor – plush red seating, huge mirrors, vintage prints and a striped ceiling. The Big Mamma Group has a few other branches across London including *Gloria* in Shoreditch, *Circolo Popolare* in Fitzrovia and *Jacuzzi* in Kensington. **£££**

The Barbary 16 Neal's Yard, WC2, www.thebarbary.co.uk. A horseshoe-shaped counter wraps around a small kitchen, where chefs rustle up north African-inspired dishes like octopus tentacle with pomegranate molasses and neck of pata negra pork. The naan e Barbari is divine, especially slathered in smoky baba ganoush. **£££**

Cork & Bottle 44–6 Cranbourn Street, WC2, www.thecorkandbottle.co.uk. An excellent retreat from Leicester Square, this casual basement wine bar offers decent food and a notable selection of wines. **££**

The Ivy 1–5 West Street, WC2, www.ivycollection.com. If you succeed in getting a reservation at this, one of London's most famous haunts (reserve well in advance, although you may have more luck at lunchtime), you'll enjoy a surprisingly unaffected atmosphere, friendly service, a familiar menu (predominantly English with international favourites) and a strong wine list. **££££**

Rules 35 Maiden Lane, WC2, www.rules.co.uk. London's oldest restaurant (est. 1798), *Rules* has a traditional menu and beautifully decorated, old-fashioned dining room with wood panelling and Art Nouveau stained glass. The robust food is very English, with beef from *Rules*' own estate in the Pennines plus lamb and a variety of game. **££££**

MAYFAIR AND ST JAMES'S

L'Autre 5b Shepherd Street, W1, www.lautrerestaurant.co.uk. Tucked away in the heart of Shepherd Market, this quaint half-timbered restaurant offers an odd combination of Polish and Mexican food that works surprisingly well. **£££**

Benares 12a Berkeley Square House, Berkeley Square, W1, www.benaresrestaurant.com. Atul Kochhar's Michelin-starred *Benares* serves sumptuous Indian dishes including smoked tandoori lamb cutlets, rogan jus and Kashmiri chilli turnips. Reservations essential. **£££**

Bentley's Oyster Bar & Grill 11–15 Swallow Street, W1, www.bentleys.org. With 100-plus years under its belt – the past 20 under the helm of chef Richard Corrigan – this Mayfair icon is synonymous with oysters (freshly shucked or creatively cooked), although its other seafood, fish and steak dishes are just as impressive. **£££**

The Diamond Jubilee Tea Salon 4th floor, Fortnum and Mason, 181 Piccadilly, W1, www.fortnumandmason.com. Opened by Queen Elizabeth II in her Jubilee year, 2012, this attractive restaurant is one of the best, and most expensive, places to have a proper afternoon tea. More than just cucumber sandwiches and cake, here you can sample smoked salmon and coronation chicken finger sandwiches and a wide range of patisserie. **££££**

Veeraswamy Victory House, 99–101 Regent St, W1, www.veeraswamy.com. London's oldest Indian restaurant, awarded a Michelin star in 2016, offers an adventurous menu combining North and South Indian cooking. **££££**

The Wolseley 160 Piccadilly, W1, www.thewolseley.com. Always busy, always glamorous, *The Wolseley* is the place to come for breakfast, afternoon tea and pre-theatre meals as well as lunch or dinner. **£££**

BLOOMSBURY AND MARYLEBONE

Berners Tavern 10 Berners Street, W1, www.bernerstavern.com. Michelin-starred chef Jason Atherton is the man behind the menu at *Berners Tavern*, the painting-adorned restaurant of the *London Edition* hotel. The seasonal menu may include rack of Herdwick lamb or roasted Dover sole. **£££**

Hoppers 77 Wigmore Street, W1, www.hopperslondon.com. The sister restaurant to *Hoppers* branches in Soho and King's Cross, the Marylebone outpost of this popular Sri Lankan haunt offers the same delicious egg hopper (fermented-rice and coconut milk pancake) and a range of roti, dosa and Tamil-style curries. **££**

Italia Uno 91 Charlotte Street, tel: 020 7637 5326. Excellent no-frills Italian sandwich shop, with walls adorned with old Italian football shirts, and football on the TV at the back. The sandwiches are what dreams are made of with fillings from grilled aubergines, artichoke and sundried tomato to mortadella and cheese, all dressed with salad and a generous drizzle of olive oil. Perfect for a quick-stop, quality lunch. **£**

Locanda Locatelli 8 Seymour Street, W1, www.locandalocatelli.com. Tucked away off Regent Street in the *Hyatt Regency* hotel is this Michelin-starred restaurant, where Giorgio Locatelli conjures up magical Italian dishes. **££££**

Orrery 55 Marylebone High Street, W1, www.orrery-restaurant.co.uk. This beautiful dining room with Art Deco features is a popular spot. Stunning, classic French dishes, intensely flavoured mains, prize-winning cheese trolley, memorable soufflés and a definitive wine list. Rooftop terrace too. **££££**

Oscar Bar and Restaurant Charlotte Street Hotel, 15–17 Charlotte Street, W1, www.firmdalehotels.com. Behind an elegant facade of Georgian townhouses is the *Charlotte Street Hotel*, whose ground-floor restaurant is a busy, vibrant place, with walls brightly painted with scenes of twenty-first-century London. A great breakfast spot, but also popular for lunch with media types. **£££**

Pied à Terre 34 Charlotte Street, W1, www.pied-a-terre.co.uk. Long-standing Michelin-starred restaurant offering dishes such as Norfolk quail, venison saddle or truffled eggs, with a range of tasting menus, including a plant-based option. **££££**

Salt Yard 54 Goodge Street, W1, www.saltyard.co.uk. Tapas restaurant inspired by the flavours of Spain and Italy, with inventive options such as courgette flowers stuffed with goats' cheese. Charcuterie and bar snacks available too. **££**

THE SOUTH BANK

Butlers Wharf Chop House Butlers Wharf Building, 36e Shad Thames, SE1, www.chophouse-restaurant.co.uk. Carnivores should go straight for the steak sandwich, served with red-wine gravy, mustard butter and fries. There are also a few fish dishes. **£££**

fish! 9 Cathedral Street, SE1, www.fishkitchen.com. Located in the shadow of Southwark Cathedral, this all-glass restaurant serves a great range of fresh and simple dishes. Great fish and chips from here and the takeaway kiosk just outside. **£££**

Mesón Don Felipe 53 The Cut, SE1, www.mesondonfelipe.co.uk. Londoners in the know flock to this excellent tapas bar. Tables fill up fast, but there's often room at the bar. A guitarist sometimes performs from a raised alcove. **££**

Oblix Level 32, The Shard, 31 St Thomas Street, SE1, www.oblixrestaurant.com. There are several upscale restaurants inside The Shard, all in the eye-wateringly expensive category (although dining in the building will save you the tower's entrance fee). This 32nd-floor one, from German restaurateur Rainer Becker (of *Zuma* and *Roka* fame), offers spectacular views and New York Grill-style food. **££££**

Oma 2–4 Bedale Street, SE1, www.oma.london. Opened in 2024, this exciting new addition to Borough Market, in a stylish, pared-back industrial setting, offers an impressive menu of fine and flavoursome food inspired by the Greek islands. **£££**

Oxo Tower Oxo Tower Wharf, Barge House St, SE1, www.oxotowerrestaurant.com. Some find it overpriced, but this iconic spot is still hugely popular. The biggest draw is the fabulous view of the Thames through huge windows. **££££**

Padella 6 Southwark Street, SE1, www.padella.co. A hugely popular, surprisingly inexpensive pasta bar and restaurant on the outskirts of Borough Market. Try the much-loved pici cacio e pepe. It's a small place and they don't take bookings, but you can join a 'virtual queue' via their website when you're in the area. A sister restaurant, *Trullo*, is up in Highbury. **££**

Le Pont de la Tour Butlers Wharf Building, 36d Shad Thames, SE1, www.lepontdelatour.co.uk. Butlers Wharf is Terence Conran land, *par excellence*, and the chic *Pont de la Tour* restaurant does fine French food such as *sole meunière* and glazed duck confit. The less formal bar downstairs has a Thameside terrace and specialises in seafood. **££££**

Tapas Brindisa 18–20 Southwark Street, SE1, www.brindisakitchens.com. Connected to one of the most popular stalls in Borough market, this restaurant is usually packed. Authentic tapas and a buzzing ambience, with some outside tables. Also a branch near South Kensington tube. **££**

The Anchor and Hope 36 The Cut, SE1, www.anchorandhopepub.co.uk. The menu of this popular gastropub (an enduring favourite in the area) features dishes such as roast porchetta with fennel, potted shrimp, and seven-hour lamb shoulder. Reasonable prices, hefty portions and friendly staff. **££**

KING'S CROSS AND AROUND

Arabica 7 Lewis Cubitt Walk, N1, www.arabicalondon.com. A favourite for zingy, flavoursome Middle Eastern food – from hot Beiruti falafel with hummus to honey halloumi, lamb koftes or grilled chicken with pistachio – with a Modernist interior featuring long iroko wood tables and brown tiled floors. **££**

Barrafina Coal Drops Yard, N1, www.barrafina.co.uk. Michelin-starred tapas, marble-topped dining counters, an extensive list of Spanish wines and a snaking queue of hopeful diners – this much-loved spot is one of the best Spanish restaurants in London. **£££**

Dishoom 5 Stable Street, N1, www.dishoom.com. There's a reason this beloved Indian restaurant is such a hit. This iconic branch (there are a few dotted across the city) is located in a grand, former railway station and offers cosy, dimly-lit, industrial surroundings. Try their signature Black Daal or the Ruby Chicken. **££**

Granary Square Brasserie 1 Granary Square, N1, www.ivycollection.com. Part of the Ivy Collection, this fancy brasserie, housed in a listed brick building, serves a host of British classics and familiar international dishes in a beautiful setting with art prints, plush furniture, chandeliers and brass décor. **£££**

Lina Stores 20 Stable Street, N1, www.linastores.co.uk**.** An exceptionally pretty Italian restaurant and delicatessen just behind Granary Square. Eat in or take away, you should visit to stock up on olive oil and antipasti, if nothing else. **££**

Mildreds 200 Pentonville Road, N1, www.mildreds.co.uk. Imaginative vegetarian and vegan cooking served in retro, café-style surroundings. Branches also in Soho, Camden and Dalston. **££**

THE CITY AND EAST LONDON

Beigel Bake 159 Brick Lane, E1, www.bricklanebeigel.co.uk. Probably London's most famous bagel shop, open 24hrs. The queues are unbelievable at peak times but the bagels– try the salt beef with gherkins and mustard, or smoked salmon with cream cheese – are more than worth it. **£**

BRAT 4 Redchurch Street, E1, www.bratrestaurant.co.uk. Exceptional Michelin-starred restaurant on the first floor of a pub, serving rustic, smoky, wood-fired food inspired by the Basque Country. **££££**

Cafe Below St Mary le Bow, Cheapside, EC2, www.cafebelow.co.uk. Situated in the atmospheric crypt of St Mary le Bow church is this excellent café/restaurant, offering a good range of tasty breakfast and lunch options. **£**

Eagle 159 Farringdon Road, EC1, www.theeaglefarringdon.co.uk. This was the pub that launched a thousand gastropubs over 30 years ago with its pioneering menu of inventive dishes. The food has a Mediterranean bias and there is a good choice of European beers. **££**

Luca 88 St John Street, EC1, www.luca.restaurant. This modern Italian restaurant, Michelin-starred in 2023 and sister of the *The Clove Club* in nearby

Shoreditch, serves expertly crafted seasonal dishes such as tagliarini with Mazara prawns and bergamot. **££££**

Lyle's 56 Shoreditch High Street, E1, www.lyleslondon.com. The first venture of chef James Lowe (of *Noma* and *St John*), Michelin-starred *Lyle's* is an airy, Scandi-style spot in a former tea factory. The menu varies, but its Modern British offerings may include white asparagus, fresh fish or Yorkshire game. **££££**

Madison One New Change, EC4, www.madisonlondon.net. In addition to upmarket stores, the One New Change shopping centre houses a cluster of bars and restaurants, including this one, which is impressively set on the rooftop, with great views of St Paul's. **£££**

Moro 34–6 Exmouth Market, EC1, www.moro.co.uk. Located on the shabby-chic Exmouth Market, this laid-back restaurant serves Moorish cuisine, where lamb is charcoal grilled, tuna is wind-dried, lemon sole wood-roasted, and manzanilla sherry partners prawns and garlic. **£££**

Silo Unit 7 Queen's Yard, White Post Lane, E9, www.silolondon.com. Pioneering *Silo* is the world's first zero waste restaurant – with a philosophy built on working without bins, using natural, whole ingredients in their cooking, and incorporating processes of fermentation, regenerative farming and other environmentally friendly methods all the way down the supply chain. It's an innovative feat – they hold a Michelin Green Star for exceptional sustainable practices. **££££**

St John Bread & Wine 94–96 Commercial Street, E1, www.stjohnrestaurant.com. Located opposite Spitalfields Market, this foodie favourite is celebrated for its 'nose-to-tail' eating. Fergus Henderson's kitchen offers simple, bold, often quirky dishes. The more expensive sister restaurant, *St John Bar Smithfield*, is a stone's throw from Smithfield's meat market. **££**

Smiths of Smithfield 67–77 Charterhouse Street, EC1, www.smithsofsmithfield.co.uk. Brunch on a weekend is really good fun in this vast post-industrial complex. Upstairs, a more refined experience is on offer in the restaurant along with views over Smithfield Market. **££**

Tayyabs 83–9 Fieldgate Street, E1, www.tayyabs.co.uk. There's frequently a queue outside this family-run Punjabi restaurant, and once you sample the mouth-watering authentic cuisine you'll understand why. The atmosphere is lively and the prices are low. The karahi lamb is a particular highlight. They don't sell alcohol, but diners are invited to bring their own. **££**

KENSINGTON, CHELSEA AND THE SOUTH

Bluebird 350 King's Road, SW3, www.bluebird-restaurant.co.uk. The emphasis at this skylit restaurant, café and bar is on seasonal ingredients. It's a posh and popular Chelsea haunt (and features occasionally on the reality TV show *Made in Chelsea*), especially good for brunch on sunny days when you can sit out in the courtyard. **£££**

Claude Bosi at Bibendum Michelin House, 81 Fulham Road, SW3, https://claudebosi.com. Formerly Sir Terence Conran's flagship restaurant, *Bibendum* reopened in 2017 with renowned chef Claude Bosi at the helm. Enjoy faultless modern European cuisine under the beautiful stained-glass windows of the former French tyre company. There's also an oyster bar downstairs. **££££**

Dinner by Heston Blumenthal Mandarin Oriental Hyde Park, 66 Knightsbridge, www.dinnerbyheston.com. Bespectacled scientist-superchef Heston Blumenthal works his usual eye-popping magic at his two-Michelin-starred London restaurant with experimental takes on historic British dishes from the fourteenth to the nineteenth centuries.

The 'meat fruit' (chicken mousse fashioned like a fruit) is of particular note; his mains include such delights as spiced pigeon with ale and artichokes. **££££**

Fifth Floor, Harvey Nichols 109–25 Knightsbridge, SW1, www.harveynichols.com. This elegant restaurant at the top of the department store has an excellent reputation. Patisseries and puddings are made on the day, and starters and main courses are always enticing. **£££**

Honest Burgers 24 Thurloe Street, SW7, www.honestburgers.co.uk. When it comes to *Honest*, if you know, you know. They make their burgers from scratch, and pride themselves on regenerative farming methods and sourcing ingredients locally (and serve the tastiest double-cooked rosemary salted chips). This location makes for an affordable stop in the South Kensington area. **£**

Kinoya Harrods, 87 Brompton Road, SW, www.harrods.com. Opened in 2023 in the luxury renovated Harrods Dining Hall, this ramen bar, serving punchy, steaming bowls of the beloved Japanese noodle dish, is an offshoot of Chef Neha Mishra's esteemed flagship *Kinoya* restaurant in Dubai – voted one of the World's 50 Best Restaurants. **£££**

Ottolenghi 63 Ledbury Road, Notting Hill, W11, www.ottolenghi.co.uk. This deli became immensely popular upon opening in 2002 by Israeli-British chef, Yotam Ottolenghi. It gained a huge following and spurred a few inventive restaurants across London, as well as several best-selling cookbooks. Fresh, flavoursome, fabulous food is made on the premises – sit at the communal table or take away. **££**

VQ Chelsea 325 Fulham Road, SW10, www.vqrestaurants.com. As its name implies, this restaurant serves good hot meals 24 hours a day, with a licence to serve alcohol to match. It's particularly popular among the trendy, well-heeled Kensington locals. **££**

Travel essentials

PRACTICAL INFORMATION

Accessible travel **135**
Accommodation **135**
Airports **136**
Apps **138**
Budgeting for your trip **138**
Climate **139**
Crime and safety **139**
Driving **140**
Electricity **141**
Embassies and consulates **141**
Emergencies **141**
Getting to London **141**
Guided tours **142**
Health and medical care **143**
LGBTQI+ travellers **144**
Money **144**
Opening hours **144**
Public holidays **144**
Telephones **145**
Time zones **145**
Tipping **145**
Toilets **145**
Tourist information **146**
Transport **146**
Visas and entry requirements **147**

ACCESSIBLE TRAVEL

London has not always been well equipped for travellers with disabilities, but it is becoming increasingly so. Buses are wheelchair accessible, and more than a third of tube stations have step-free access – they're marked with a blue symbol on the tube map and are announced on the tube itself. There are surprisingly few public toilets in London, but all mainline train stations and major tube stations have them (although you may have to pay to use them). Department stores, free museums and galleries are other good options, and almost always have an accessible toilet. Many London car hire companies can provide a range of wheelchair-friendly and adapted vehicles.

A helpful source of information is the Transport for London (TfL) website, which has an accessible journey planner, accessibility maps and guides (www.tfl.gov.uk). The Visit London website (www.visitlondon.com) also has information about accessible hotels, attractions and entertainment venues. Tourism for All (www.tourismforall.co.uk) offers useful advice and AccessAble (www.accessable.co.uk) is a comprehensive online resource listing the access provisions and facilities for different sites, including hotels, shops, attractions and arts and entertainment venues.

ACCOMMODATION

London has a wide range of accommodation, but bargains are hard to come by, so it's important to book ahead as London fills up in the summer.

While accommodation is generally fairly expensive for what you get, there are a few hotels offering affordable accommodation in a central location. Many of these belong to mid-range chains such as Travelodge (www.travelodge.co.uk) or Premiere Inn (www.premierinn.com), in convenient areas such as the South Bank and the City.

In general, hotels in the West End and Mayfair tend to be expensive, with plenty of upmarket options but little choice at the lower end of the scale. The Bloomsbury/Marylebone area to the north is a clever option – it's central and characterful, but prices are more reasonable. There are some delightfully old-fashioned hotels in Victoria, and the streets close to the station are full of terraced B&B accommodation. There are also streets full of townhouse hotels in Kensington and Chelsea, offering dependable comfort in the middle-to-upper price bracket.

Alternatively, a good range of slightly cheaper accommodation can be found outside of central London, in areas like Putney and the South West, around Greenwich and the South East, or just outside North London, which are all well connected via tubes and buses and are great locations in themselves, with their own charm.

If you arrive without a reservation, head for a Tourist Information Centre (see page 146) or search Visit London's accommodation booking service at www.visitlondon.com.

Short-term home rental companies like Airbnb (www.airbnb.co.uk) offer local, often relatively cheap accommodation in excellent locations, and you might be able to get a good deal on different types of accommodation on comparison sites like Booking.com (www.booking.com).

AIRPORTS

London is served by six airports: the two major hubs are Heathrow and Gatwick, while Stansted, Luton (both north of the centre) and London City are primarily for chartered, budget or short-haul flights. There's also London Southend, 40miles (64km) away southeast, which has a connecting train to the centre.

Heathrow (tel: 0344 335 1801; www.heathrow.com) is 15 miles (24km) west of central London. The fastest connection from the airport to central London is the Heathrow Express (www.heathrowexpress.com) to Paddington Station, which takes 15 minutes and runs every 15 minutes between 5.10am and 11.25pm. The fare is a hefty £25 single at peak times and £39 return. Alternatively, you can get the Elizabeth line to Paddington, which runs all the way from Reading to Liverpool Street, Shenfield and Abbey Wood in the east. It takes around 26 minutes from Paddington, runs between 5.21am and midnight and fares start from £12.80. There is also a direct Underground route on the Piccadilly Line, which reaches the West End in around 50 minutes. It operates from 5am until 11.30pm daily and all through the night on Fridays and Saturdays, fares start from £5.50. National Express (tel: 0371 781 8178; www.nationalexpress.com) runs coaches from Heathrow day and night; the fastest service takes around 25 minutes to Earl's Court, depending on traffic, and fares start from £8.40.

Heathrow is well-served by taxis and services like Uber; a ride in a London 'black cab' into town will cost upwards of £70 plus tip, and take 30–60 minutes, depending on traffic.

Gatwick (tel: 0344 892 0322; www.gatwickairport.com) is 27 miles (43km) south of London. The airport isn't on the Underground network, but the Gatwick Express (tel: 0345 850 1530; www.gatwickexpress.com) runs every 15 minutes from London Victoria Station between 5am–11pm. The train takes 30 minutes and costs upwards of £20.50 one-way (slightly cheaper online). Southern also runs services from Gatwick to Victoria, with similar hours and prices. Thameslink trains run direct services from Gatwick to Blackfriars, City Thameslink, Farringdon and St Pancras International, with an average journey time of 30 minutes (from around £20 one way).

easyBus (www.easybus.com) run services from Gatwick to West London while National Express bus services (www.nationalexpress.com) operate the 32-mile (51km) journey between Heathrow and Gatwick (£22 single), taking between 60 and 90 minutes.

Stansted (tel: 0808 169 7031; www.stanstedairport.com) is located 34 miles (54km) northeast of London. The Stansted Express (tel: 0345-748 4950; www.stanstedexpress.com) leaves for Liverpool Street station every 15 minutes from 5.30am until 0.30am and from Liverpool Street to Stansted between 3.40am (Mon, Fri and Sat), 4.10am (Sun) or 4.40am (Tue–Thu) and 11.25pm, and costs £23.90 one way; the journey takes around 45 minutes.

The National Express Coach (www.nationalexpress.com) leaves for Victoria Station around every 15 minutes, 24 hours a day, takes around 90 minutes and costs from £11 one way. There are also services to Southwark, Paddington and Waterloo.

The easyBus (www.easybus.com) runs every 30 minutes 24 hours a day, daily, between Stansted and Victoria bus station; single fares go from £12. Journey time is 1 hour 50 minutes.

Taxis cost around £80.

London City Airport (tel: 020 7646 0000; www.londoncityairport.com) is just 6 miles (10km) east of the City and is mainly used by business travellers. The airport has its own station on the Docklands Light Railway (DLR), which connects with the Underground network at Bank station.

Luton Airport (tel: 0158 240 5100; www.london-luton.co.uk) is linked by Thameslink rail services with London St Pancras International; some trains continue to Gatwick via Blackfriars. There is a free shuttle bus between the airport and Luton train station. The journey to St Pancras takes about 45 minutes, and trains run every 10–15 minutes (hourly through the night). National Express (www.nationalexpress.com) runs coaches between Luton and Central London four times hourly, night and day, and Green Line buses (route 757) run to Victoria, twice hourly, and take about 60 minutes (www.arrivabus.co.uk/greenline).

APPS

International taxi apps such as Uber (www.uber.com) and Bolt (https://bolt.eu) are available in London, while higher-end services run with Addison Lee (www.addisonlee.com). London's famous black cabs can be hailed in the street or booked via the Gett app (www.gett.com).

Citymapper (https://citymapper.com) is a useful transport app for planning journeys, with live times.

TfL Go (www.tfl.gov.uk) is a useful app for planning accessible journeys around the city, as is AccessAble (www.accessable.co.uk).

RingGo (https://ringgo.co.uk) is a useful app for finding and paying for parking around the city.

Visit London (www.visitlondon.com), the city's official tourism website, has a handy app to help you plan and make the most of your trip.

BUDGETING FOR YOUR TRIP

In general, London is a very expensive city, so make sure you come prepared.

Accommodation. Double room in Central London, excluding breakfast, including VAT: from around £110 to over £400 per night. You might find cheap deals online, if you book in advance, or if you go for a budget chain option, there are a few dotted around the city.

Meals and drinks. For a decent sit-down breakfast, expect to pay anywhere from £9 and up; for lunch (in a pub, including one drink) around £15; for dinner at a decent restaurant (two courses, including a drink) £25 and up. Cafés, bakeries, bars, sandwich shops and food markets are cheap and cheerful options, and there are plenty of them around. A bottle of house wine costs £15–25, a pint of beer £6; a coffee £2–3.

Entertainment. A ticket to the cinema will cost around £7–15; admission to a club: £5–20; and a good seat at a West End musical can be upwards of £100 – try find cheaper deals online, in advance. Admission to many museums and art galleries is free, except for special exhibitions; others cost around £10–20. Tickets for the most expensive attractions vary wildly, but many are available '2FOR1' if you travel by rail (see www.daysoutguide.co.uk). The London Pass (https://londonpass.com) could save you money if you're planning to visit multiple attractions.

CLIMATE

The weather in the capital is generally mild compared with the rest of the country, with the warming effects of the city itself keeping off the worst of the cold in winter. Temperatures below freezing do not tend to be prolonged, with January temperatures averaging 8°C (46.6°F). Maximum temperatures in the summer months average 24°C (75.2°F), but they can soar to well over 30°C (86°F), causing the city to become stiflingly hot. In recent years, temperatures have stayed in the 30s for weeks at a time throughout the summer.

However, temperatures can fluctuate considerably from day to day, and surprise showers catch people unawares all year round. This unpredictability has its plus side – Brits characteristically love to complain about the weather. Unsuspecting visitors should come prepared with wet-weather clothes and a brolly, whatever the season; layers are sensible.

CRIME AND SAFETY

Serious crime is low for a city of this size. It is generally a safe city, but like any big city there are some areas which could be more dangerous, and you should watch out for pickpockets in busy spots (any busy central streets and markets in particular). Take the usual precautions, but in the event of a theft or crime call 101 for non-emergencies, 999 for emergencies. The threat of terrorism in recent decades has led to an increased police presence around major buildings. Police, identifiable by their black uniforms and high-rise hats, are usually unarmed and, on the whole, friendly and helpful.

DRIVING

If you are only staying a short while in London, don't hire a car. Negotiating Central London by car is stressful for the uninitiated, due to the city's web of one-way streets, bad signposting and impatient drivers, not to mention expense due to the Congestion charge.

If a car is a necessity or you want to explore further afield, you should drive on the left and observe speed limits (police detection cameras are numerous). It is illegal to drink and drive, and penalties are severe. Drivers and passengers (back and front) are legally obliged wear seat belts.

Congestion charge/ULEZ. Cars driving into a clearly marked Congestion Charge zone between 7am and 6pm Mon–Fri, and 12–6pm Sat–Sun, are charged £15. The Ultra Low Emission Zone (ULEZ) imposes an additional charge on vehicles which don't conform to certain emissions standards. See https://tfl.gov.uk/modes/driving for details on charge areas (with a vehicle checker and postcode checker), and details on how to pay fees.

Speed limits. Unless otherwise indicated these are: 30mph (50kmh) in urban areas (note that 20mph is increasingly common), 60mph (100kmh) on normal roads away from built-up areas, 70mph (112kmh) on motorways and dual carriageways.

Parking. This is a big problem in central London. Meters or pay-and-display machines are slightly less expensive than multi-storey car parks, but only allow parking for a limited number of hours; it can also be hard to find a free one. Many areas of central London operate 'pay by phone' parking only, for which you will need a credit card. RingGo (https://ringgo.co.uk) is also a useful app for finding parking spots around the city.

Breakdown. The following organisations operate 24-hour breakdown assistance: AA (tel: 0333 004 6046; www.theaa.com) and RAC (tel: 0330 159 8743; www.rac.co.uk).

Car hire. To rent a car, you must be at least 21 years old and in possession of a valid driving licence (held for at least one year) and a credit card. The cost usually includes insurance and unlimited mileage but always check this.

All the hire major companies are represented in London; most have outlets at the airports as well as in the centre.

Alamo www.alamo.co.uk; **Avis** www.avis.co.uk; **Budget** www.budget.co.uk; **Hertz** www.hertz.co.uk; **Sixt** www.sixt.co.uk.

ELECTRICITY

The standard current in Britain is 230-volt, 50 cycle AC. Plugs have three pins rather than two, so bring an adaptor as necessary.

EMBASSIES AND CONSULATES

Contact your consulate or embassy only for real emergencies, such as loss of a passport or all your money, a serious accident or trouble with the police. For a list of foreign embassies, high commissions and consulates in London, see www.gov.uk/government/publications/foreign-embassies-in-the-uk.

EMERGENCIES

For police, fire brigade or ambulance dial **999** from any telephone (no payment required).

GETTING TO LONDON

By air. There are regular flights from most major airports in the world to London. For information on the city's airports, see page 136.

By rail. The Channel Tunnel provides Eurostar (www.eurostar.com) passenger services by rail from Paris Nord (2 hrs 15 mins), Lille Europe (1 hr 20 mins), Brussels Midi (2 hrs) and Amsterdam (3 hr 40 mins) to London St Pancras.

Vehicles are carried by trains through the tunnel from Folkestone in Kent to Calais in France by LeShuttle (formerly Eurotunnel; www.leshuttle.com).

The trip takes 35 minutes, and there are two to four departures every hour. Although bookings are not essential, they are advisable at peak times. Fares are cheaper late at night or in the early morning.

By ferry. Ferries operate between many British and Continental ports. Calais–Dover is the shortest crossing (75–90 minutes). Some of the main companies are:

Brittany Ferries www.brittany-ferries.co.uk. Sails from Portsmouth to Caen, Cherbourg, Le Havre and St-Malo, Poole–Cherbourg and Plymouth–Roscoff.

DFDS Seaways www.dfds.com. Dover–Dunkirk and Dover–Calais.

P&O Ferries www.poferries.com. Dover–Calais.

By coach. Within the country, National Express (www.nationalexpress.com) runs services from Victoria Coach Station on Buckingham Palace Road.

GUIDED TOURS

Visit London (www.visitlondon.com) has comprehensive list of tours around the city, and some are including when you purchase the London Pass (https://londonpass.com).

Bus tours. Hop-on hop-off double-decker bus tour operators include the Big Bus Tours (www.bigbustours.com), Golden Tours (www.goldentours.com) and Tootbus (www.tootbus.com). Departure points include Marble Arch, Trafalgar Square, Piccadilly, Victoria and Tower Hill.

Walking tours. London Walks (www.walks.com) offers almost 100 walks, many with literary and historical themes.

Food tours. Eating Europe (www.eatingeurope.com) offers some interesting tours around different areas of the city, including Soho, the East End, and Borough Market and the Southbank. You can eat your way around the famous foodie spots whilst knowledgeable guides walk you through the unique history of the area.

Black Taxi Tours. These offer a full commentary from knowledgeable cabbies. Tours (including highlights, London by night, or themed tours) range from two to seven hours long, starting from £175 per cab. See www.blacktaxitours.co.uk for information.

River travel. Much of London's history is centred on the Thames, and seeing the city from the river provides a fascinating perspective, from lunch and dinner cruises to hop-on-hop-off tours. City Experiences (www.cityexperiences.com) serves the main piers down to Tower Pier and Greenwich; Thames River Sightseeing (www.thamesriversightseeing.com) runs from Westminster Pier to Greenwich. Circular cruises between St Katharine's and Westminster Pier are available from Crown River Cruises, Blackfriars Pier (www.crownrivercruise.co.uk). Uber Boat by Thames Clippers (www.thamesclippers.com) runs services from between Barking Riverside Pier and Putney Pier, with 24 stops along the way; they also run the Tate Boat (see page 40).

Canal trips. Jason's Trip (www.jasons.co.uk) is a traditional painted narrow boat making 45-minute trips along the Regent's Canal between Little Venice and Camden Lock. The London Waterbus Company (www.londonwaterbus.com) runs from Camden Lock to Little Venice, with discounted tickets to the zoo at Regent's Park.

HEALTH AND MEDICAL CARE

Citizens from the EU, Norway, Iceland, Liechtenstein or Switzerland will need health and travel insurance for the duration of their stay; they can receive free statutory treatment on producing a valid European Health Insurance Card (EHIC). Other countries also have reciprocal arrangements for free treatment. However, most visitors will be liable for medical and dental treatment, so will have to pay for any non-emergency treatment. Further guidance can be found here: www.gov.uk/guidance.

Major hospitals include Charing Cross Hospital (Fulham Palace Road, W6, tel: 020 3311 1234) and St Thomas's (Westminster Bridge Road, SE1, tel: 020 7188 7188). Guy's Hospital Dental Department is at St Thomas Street, SE1, tel: 020 7188 8006. For the nearest hospital or doctor's (non-emergency), tel: 111 (NHS 111). For emergencies call 999.

Late pharmacies: Boots on Piccadilly Circus is open until 11pm Mon–Sat (closes 6pm Sun), while others can be found via the 'find a pharmacy' search tool at www.nhs.uk.

LGBTQI+ TRAVELLERS

The LGBTQI+ scene in London centres around Soho and Vauxhall, with Old Compton Street in Soho offering many welcoming bars, and there are also many thriving LGBTQI+ bars and clubs in East London (see page 109). For information, advice or assistance call Switchboard, the LGBTQI+ helpline, on tel: 0800 0119 100, www.switchboard.lgbt.

MONEY

Currency. The monetary unit is the pound sterling (£), divided into 100 pence (p). Banknotes: £5, £10, £20, £50. Coins: 1p, 2p, 5p, 10p, 20p, 50p, £1, £2. Many of London's large stores also accept euros.

Currency exchange. The latest exchange rates can be found at www.xe.com. You will probably get the best rate by using an ATM (cash machine), with your bankcard from home. ATMs are all over the city but some charge withdrawal rates. Post offices and department stores have *bureaux de change* that don't charge commission. At private *bureaux de change* (some open 24 hours), rates can be very low and commissions high.

Tax refunds. These enable visitors from outside the European Union to reclaim the 20 percent value-added tax when spending over a certain amount. Stores can supply VAT refund forms, which should be presented to Customs officials when leaving the country.

OPENING HOURS

Banks: Usually Mon–Fri 9.30am–5pm, although some close at 3.30pm. Saturday-morning banking is common in shopping areas.

Shops: Most open Mon–Sat 9am–10am and close around 5.30pm to 6pm. In commercial areas such as Oxford Street shops stay open until 8pm Mon–Sat (until 9 or 10pm on Thu). On Sundays major shops are only allowed six hours of trading between 10am and 6pm.

PUBLIC HOLIDAYS

On public (or 'bank') holidays, banks and offices close, but most other amenities remain open. They are: New Year's Day (January 1), Good Friday (March/April), Easter Monday (March/April), May Day (first Monday in May), Spring Bank Holiday (last Monday in May), Summer Bank Holiday (last Monday in August), Christmas Day and Boxing Day (December 25 and 26).

TELEPHONES

London's UK dialling code is 020. To call from abroad, dial the 44 international access code for Britain, then 20, then the eight-digit number. To phone abroad, dial 00 followed by the international code for the country you want, then the number: Australia (61); Ireland (353); US and Canada (1), etc.

With the ubiquity of mobiles (cell phones), London now has fewer public phone boxes. London's iconic red phone boxes are more often used for photo opportunities. Those remaining in use accept coins and/or credit/debit cards. At coin-operated phone boxes, the smallest coin accepted is 20p; minimum call charge is 60p.

TIME ZONES

In winter (Nov–March) the UK is on Greenwich Mean Time (GMT). In summer (April–Oct) clocks are put forward one hour and the country moves to British Summer Time (BST).

TIPPING

Many restaurants automatically add a 10–15 percent service charge to your bill. It's not customary, and you can deduct this if you are not happy with the service. It is usual to tip guides, porters and cabbies about 10 percent.

TOILETS

There are surprisingly few public toilets in London, but all mainline train stations and major tube stations have them (although you may have to pay to use them). Both London King's Cross and St Pancras stations have free toilets. Department stores, free museums and galleries are other good options, and almost always have an accessible toilet. The TfL website (www.tfl.gov.uk) has information on facilities across London, and apps such as Flush or Toilet Finder are also useful.

TOURIST INFORMATION

The website for Visit London, the official tourist board, is www.visitlondon.com. It contains a huge amount of information on attractions, tours, upcoming events and festivals, as well as practical information and a hotel booking service. They also have a list of visitor information centres around London, and provide free downloadable travel maps for navigating the city.

TRANSPORT

For information on buses, Underground, Overground, DLR and trains contact Transport for London (tel: 0343 222 1234; www.tfl.gov.uk). For national rail queries, tel: 0345 748 4950, www.nationalrail.co.uk. Both websites have excellent journey planners and information on accessible travel facilities.

Oyster cards. These are smart cards that you charge up with however much you wish to pay, then touch in on card readers at tube and rail stations and on buses, so that an amount is deducted each time you use it. They cost £5 and can be bought from stations or online in advance via the TfL website. Oyster cards and contactless payment cards offer better value than buying single tickets, and travelcards valid for one, seven days, or one month, cover travel on all tube, bus, DLR and local trains (within the specified zones). A one-day, peak Travelcard (zones 1, 2, 3 and 4) costs £15.90. It's cheaper to 'pay as you go' in zones 1 and 2 with an Oyster card or contactless, as there is a daily cap limiting the fare at £8.50, no matter how many journeys you make within those zones. See https://tfl.gov.uk/fares for more information on fares and capping.

Children under 11 travel free on all transport, those aged 11–15 travel free on buses and trams with an Oyster photocard or can get half adult fare rate on the tube.

Underground. Known as the tube, this is the quickest way to get across town. During the rush hours (8am–9.30am and 5–7pm) stations and trains are packed. Services run from 5am to around midnight and all through the night on Fridays and Saturdays on some lines. If you're heading for the end of a line, your last train may leave closer to 11pm. Most lines have trains every couple of minutes at peak times and every few minutes off peak.

Docklands Light Railway (DLR). This is a fully automated railway that runs through redeveloped areas of east London and to Greenwich, and connects with the tube network at Bank, Tower Gateway, Stratford and a few other stations. Tickets and fares are the same as for the tube.

Buses. Most buses run fairly frequently from 6am–midnight or 12.30am and are then replaced by night buses (identified by an N before the number), which run every half hour or hour until dawn and usually pass through the Trafalgar Square area. Some buses run 24-hours a day. Cash is not accepted and paper tickets are no longer issued; touch in with an Oyster or contactless payment card as you board (you don't need to tap when you get off). The flat adult fare across London is £1.50.

Trains. London's principal National Rail stations are Charing Cross, Euston, King's Cross, Liverpool Street, London Bridge, Paddington, St Pancras International, Victoria and Waterloo. If you are staying in the suburbs, the fastest way into central London is often by this network, used heavily by commuters, but less packed than the tube between rush hours.

Taxis. Official black cabs display the regulated charges on the meter. You can hail a cab in the street if the orange light on its roof is on, or you will find them at railway stations, airports and taxi ranks. You can book a taxi in advance at www.tfl.gov.uk. Alternatively, book a cab or share a ride by using the smartphone apps (see page 138).

Licensed minicabs can only be booked via a registered office, either by telephone or online, so avoid any illegal ones touting for business on the street late at night. The TfL website has a useful licence checker: https://tfl.gov.uk/info-for/taxis-and-private-hire/licensing/licence-checker.

VISAS AND ENTRY REQUIREMENTS

A valid **passport** is required to enter the UK. A **visa** to visit the United Kingdom is not required by nationals of member states of the European Economic Area (EEA), the Commonwealth (including Australia, Canada, New Zealand and South Africa, as long as the stay does not exceed six months) and the USA. Nationals of other countries should check with the British Embassy or www.gov.uk and apply for a visa. For up-to-date official information on visas, visit www.gov.uk/check-uk-visa.

Index

10 Downing Street 37

A
Albert Memorial 81
Anchor Inn 67
Apsley House Art
　Collection 79

B
Bank of England 75
Bankside Gallery 64
Banqueting House 37
Barbican 74, 106
BFI London IMAX Cinema 63
BFI Southbank 62
Big Ben 39
Borough 105
Borough Market 68
Brick Lane 91
British Library 57
British Museum 55
Buckingham Palace 50
Burlington Arcade 54
Butlers Wharf 71

C
Camden 89, 104
Canary Wharf 92
Cenotaph 37
Changing the Guard 50
Charing Cross Road 102
Chelsea Physic Garden 87
Cheyne Walk 87
Chinatown 45
Churchill War Rooms 38
City Hall 70
Cleopatra's Needle 49
Clink Prison Museum 67
Columbia Road 104
Cork Street 54
County Hall 61
Courtauld Institute of Art
　Gallery 49
Covent Garden 45, 102
Crown Jewels 77
Cutty Sark 95

D
Dennis Severs' House 91
Dr Samuel Johnson's
　House 72
Dulwich 96
Dulwich Picture Gallery 97

F
Fortnum & Mason 52, 102
Freud Museum 90

G
Gabriel's Wharf 64
Golden Hinde 67
Green Park 50
Greenwich 94
Greenwich Park 95
Guildhall 75

H
Ham House 98
Hamley's 112
Hampstead 89
Hampstead Heath 89
Hampton Court Palace 99
Harrods 85
Harvey Nichols 86
Hay's Galleria 70
Hayward Gallery 62
Highgate 90
HMS Belfast 70
Holland Park 82
Horniman Museum 97
Horse Guards 37
Hoxton 91
Hyde Park 79
Hyde Park Corner 78

I
Imperial War Museum 63
Institute of Contemporary
　Arts 51

K
Kensington High Street 81
Kensington Palace 81
Kenwood House 89
Kew 98
King's Gallery 50
King's Road 86, 103
Knightsbridge 103

L
Lawn Tennis Museum 98
Leadenhall Market 76
Leicester Square 45
Leighton House 82
Lloyd's of London 76
London Dungeon 61
London Eye 62
London Transport
　Museum 47
London Zoo 58
Lord's Cricket Ground 58

M
Madame Tussaud's 59

INDEX

Mansion House 75
Marble Arch 79
Market Hall 46
Marylebone High Street 103
Mayfair 53
Millennium Bridge 65
Monument 77
Museum of London 74
Museum of London Docklands 92

N

National Army Museum 87
National Gallery 34
National Maritime Museum 95
National Portrait Gallery 35
National Theatre 63, 105
Natural History Museum 83
Nelson's Column 34
New Bond Street 54, 103
Notting Hill 103

O

O2 Arena 94
Old Bond Street 54, 103
Old Operating Theatre and Herb Garret 68
Old Royal Naval College 96
Old Vic 105
Old Vic Theatre 63
One New Change 103
Oxford Street 43, 101
OXO Tower 64

P

Palace of Westminster 38
Pall Mall 52
Piccadilly 52
Piccadilly Circus 42
Planetarium 95

Poets' Corner 40
Portobello Road 104
Portobello Road Market 82
Primrose Hill 89

Q

Queen Elizabeth Olympic Park 93
Queen's House 96

R

Regent's Park 58
Regent Street 42, 102
Richmond Park 98
Rose Theatre 67
Royal Academy of Arts 53
Royal Albert Hall 81, 106
Royal Botanic Gardens 98
Royal Courts of Justice 72
Royal Court Theatre 105
Royal Festival Hall 62, 106
Royal Hospital 87
Royal Observatory 95
Royal Opera House 47, 107

S

Sadler's Wells 89
Sambourne House 82
Science Museum 84
Sea Life London Aquarium 61
Serpentine 80
Shakespeare's Globe 66, 106
Shard, The 68
Shepherd Market 52
Sherlock Holmes Museum 59
Sir John Soane's Museum 72
Sloane Street 86
Soho 44, 102

Somerset House 48
Southbank Centre 62
Southwark Cathedral 68
Spitalfields 104
Spitalfields Market 90
St James's 51
St James's Church 52
St James's Palace 51
St James's Park 50
St James's Square 52
St Martin-in-the-Fields 35
St Mary-le-Strand 48
St Pancras Station 56
St Paul's Cathedral 73
Strand 48
St Stephen Walbrook 75

T, V

Tate Britain 40
Tate Modern 64
the Sky Garden 75
Tottenham Court Road 102
Tower Bridge 70
Tower of London 77
Trafalgar Square 33
Victoria & Albert Museum 84

W, Y

Wallace Collection 59
Wellcome Collection 58
Wellington Arch 78
Westminster Abbey 39
Westminster Cathedral 40
Whitechapel Art Gallery 91
Wigmore Hall 59, 106
Wimbledon Common 98
Winchester Palace 67
Wren, Christopher 73
Young Vic Theatre 63
Young V&A 112

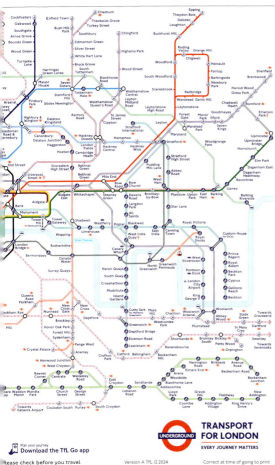

152 CREDITS

THE MINI ROUGH GUIDE TO
LONDON

First Edition 2025

Editor: Beth Williams
Author: Libby Davies
Picture Manager: Tom Smyth
Cartography Update: Katie Bennett
Layout: Grzegorz Madejak
Production Operations Manager: Katie Bennett
Publishing Technology Manager: Rebeka Davies
Head of Publishing: Sarah Clark
Photography Credits: Lisa Clarimont 21; Lydia Evans/Apa Publications 61, 63, 70, 88, 96, 99; Ming Tang-Evans/Apa Publications 24, 53, 57, 59, 86, 91, 93, 107; Peter Smith/St Pauls Cathedral 73; Public domain 22, 27; Shutterstock 1, 6, 8, 11, 12TL, 12CL, 12BL, 12CR, 12BR, 12TR, 13CT, 13CB, 13B, 13T, 14T, 14BL, 14CR, 16T, 16CL, 16BL, 16CR, 18T, 18CL, 18B, 18CR, 28, 30, 32, 34, 37, 38, 41, 43, 44, 47, 48, 51, 55, 65, 66, 69, 74, 76, 79, 80, 83, 85, 94, 100, 102, 104, 108, 111, 113, 117, 119, 120; Stefan Johnson 115; The Wolseley 14CL
Cover Credits: Big Ben **Shutterstock**

About the author
Libby Davies is a travel editor at Rough Guides. London-based, she still finds the city just as exciting as when she first moved in 2016. She grew up in Yorkshire and still spends time walking around the gorgeous peaks, dales and reservoirs of the north. She has updated guidebooks to London and Spain, and wherever she is travelling she likes to seek out books by local authors, especially novels that help conjure a sense of place.

Distribution
UK, Ireland and Europe: Apa Publications (UK) Ltd; sales@roughguides.com
United States and Canada: Ingram Publisher Services; ips@ingramcontent.com
Australia and New Zealand: Booktopia; retailer@booktopia.com.au
Worldwide: Apa Publications (UK) Ltd; sales@roughguides.com

Special Sales, Content Licensing and CoPublishing
Rough Guides can be purchased in bulk quantities at discounted prices. We can create special editions, personalised jackets and corporate imprints tailored to your needs. sales@roughguides.com; http://roughguides.com

All Rights Reserved
© 2025 Apa Digital AG
License edition © Apa Publications Ltd UK

Printed in Czech Republic

This book was produced using **Typefi** automated publishing software.

No part of this book may be reproduced, stored in a retrieval system or transmitted in any form or means electronic, mechanical, photocopying, recording or otherwise, without prior written permission from Apa Publications.

Contact us
Every effort has been made to provide accurate information in this publication, but changes are inevitable. The publisher cannot be held responsible for any resulting loss, inconvenience or injury sustained by any traveller as a result of information or advice contained in the guide. We would appreciate it if readers would call our attention to any errors or outdated information, or if you feel we've left something out. Please send your comments with the subject line "Rough Guide Mini London Update" to mail@uk.roughguides.com.